LEADING
Muslims
TO JESUS

A PRACTICAL GUIDE

by Christi Trimbur

Copyright © 2018 Live Dead Publishing.
ALL RIGHTS RESERVED.

Published by Live Dead Publishing
1445 N. Boonville Ave, Springfield, Missouri 65802

Cover design, typesetting, and interior design by Prodigy Pixel (www.prodigypixel.com).

No portion of this book may be reproduced, stored in a retrieval system, or transmitted in any form or by any means—electronic, mechanical, photocopy, recording, or any other—except for brief quotations in printed reviews, without the prior written permission of the publisher.

Unless otherwise specified, Scripture quotations used in this book are from from The Holy Bible, English Standard Version. ESV® Text Edition: 2016. Copyright © 2001 by Crossway Bibles, a publishing ministry of Good News Publishers. Used by permission. All rights reserved.

ISBN-13: 978-0-9981789-5-0

Printed in the United States of America

TABLE OF CONTENTS

Foreword — 7
Preface — 11

PART ONE: SHARING WITH MUSLIMS — 14

Chapter 1: *Know Their Content and Then Know Their Story* — 16
Chapter 2: *Start with a Divine Mandate* — 30
Chapter 3: *Engage in Intentional Interaction* — 36
Chapter 4: *Relinquish Your Power and Embrace Your Need* — 40
Chapter 5: *Take Risks to Reach Out* — 44
Chapter 6: *Develop Reciprocity and Interdependence* — 48
Chapter 7: *Go Beyond the Superficial* — 54
Chapter 8: *Be Authentic and Transparent in Worship* — 60
Chapter 9: *Make a Life-Changing Decision* — 66
Chapter 10: *Take Action to Be Counter-Cultural* — 70
Chapter 11: *Be a Bridge Builder* — 74

PART TWO: MOVING FORWARD — 78

Chapter 12: *Go and Make Disciples* — 80
Chapter 13: *Church Planting* — 86
Chapter 14: *The Insider Movement* — 94

Conclusion — 102

Appendix A: *Evangelism Journal Entry* — 108
Appendix B: *Discipleship Tracking Chart* — 113
Endnotes — 116
Sources & Recommended Reading — 119
Acknowledgements — 121

FOREWORD

Christi and Adam Trimbur believe in missions because they want to go home. Full of joy as they are, they have also walked the road of sorrow both personally and professionally. They know by experience that we are pilgrims and strangers, that this world is not our home. They understand that to go home we must obey Christ's commission to make disciples of all unreached peoples (Matt. 28:19–20) and that this gospel of the kingdom must be preached in all the world among every people group and then the end will come (24:14). The Trimburs understand that leading Muslims to Jesus is both our joy and our obedience, and it holds the promise of home-going when the work is done.

The Trimbur trail has wound from the West Bank to Syria to Jordan to Egypt. All along the way they sought to lead Muslims to Jesus. Jesus doesn't love Muslims more than atheists, Hindus, Buddhists, or any lost human—all are precious in His sight. Yet these are the facts: Islam is an active, missionary religion; Islamic expansion is organized and well-funded; Islam's center is the Middle East, the locus of world history; and Muslims now number around 1.7 billion globally. Almost one of every four humans alive today is Muslim. We all want to go home, and the Trimburs want to see many of their Muslim friends (and yours) with us in heaven. If the gospel is to be preached globally, then there certainly must be a priority on preaching to Muslims.

This book was written from the desire to go home, from the realization that homecoming depends on missions going and from the awakening among Christians towards Muslims that God is bringing to our own homes and havens. In the West and around the globe it is now impossible not to be graced with meeting Muslims everywhere—stores, schools, offices, and neighborhoods. God in His sovereignty both sends us to Muslim lands to share His great love and lovingly brings Muslims to our homelands that they might hear about our Savior and have opportunity to receive Him as Master and Lord.

Christi Trimbur has written a delightful, practical book geared at helping women and men love Muslims to Jesus wherever they live. This book is intended to help those who encounter Muslims daily to naturally and intentionally share biblical truth and hope with them. Drawing on her experience in the Arab world, Christi gives simple, doable advice on how we can lovingly invite Muslims to be freed from sin and assured of their heavenly home.

The gospel isn't that complicated, but it is hard. It does demand death to self and to false thinking. It is not easy to win Muslims to Jesus, but it is worth it for twin beauties. First and foremost, Jesus is so beautiful, and secondly, so are Muslims. Muslims are beautiful. They are created in the image of God, and He desires many Muslims to be saved and become part of His family.

For all of you who see the beauty of Muslims that God brings into your life, this book is a practical resource to show you how to go beyond shy waves and smiles to open hearts and homes, to faithful and winsome gospel proclamation, to making disciples of Muslim friends, to loving Muslims to Jesus.

I'm glad you have it. I long with Christi and Adam to go home. Let us invite as many Muslims as we can to go with us.

DICK BROGDEN
Cairo, Egypt
Founder of the Live Dead Movement

PREFACE

"Behold, I am doing a new thing; now it springs forth, do you not perceive it? I will make a way in the wilderness and rivers in the desert."

Isaiah 43:19

I have spent most of my adult life in the Arab world with the sole purpose of sharing the gospel with Muslims. Nothing gives me greater joy than to see a Muslim's heart begin to be unveiled as she starts to see Jesus. It's a beautiful privilege for which I am so very thankful.

That being said, Muslim ministry is hard, almost impossible without the divine intervention of the Holy Spirit. Over the years, I have learned one thing through ministering to Muslims: I cannot save anyone nor can I plant a single church. That work belongs to the Lord. My sole obligation is to obey Jesus immediately and completely.

The Lord has a funny way of continually teaching me this lesson. A few years ago, I found myself in a huge Arab city asking the Lord for inroads into the lives of Arab women in my neighborhood. I committed complete obedience to His leading once again. In the quiet of my prayer room, I told the Lord I would do whatever it took to see His gospel proclaimed among Arab Muslims. It seems the Lord took me up on my offer.

The Holy Spirit quickened my heart to enter a shop in a very creepy mall by our apartment. I was a bit reticent to go in because it was dark and scary, but taking a deep breath, I walked in. And with that began a beautiful relationship with several women working in a couple of the shops. On one of my visits, I brought a new missionary with me. I assured her we would just be drinking tea and I would tell the next Bible story. No big deal. Just sharing Jesus' story with Muslims. Only on this particular day, the ladies weren't ready to hear my story when we arrived. They were eating some of the foulest smelling fish I have ever encountered. They insisted we try some. I tried to decline. I used every excuse I could think of. I tried to help my friend out of it. And just as I opened my mouth to refuse the "delicacy" once more, a hand shot into my mouth and dropped the salty meat on my tongue. All I could do was pray, "Lord, help me keep this down." I gulped and teary-eyed looked over at my friend who was not at all happy with her mouthful. However, once we both swallowed, we were able to share the gospel story with a group of ladies who had never heard it. It seems to me that having to eat gross fish is a small price to pay for that.

Ministering among Muslims is not for the faint of heart. It requires a tenacity to continue going when it seems all hope is lost. It requires faith beyond human ability. It requires a complete death to self in order that Jesus might be glorified. It requires obeying Jesus completely and immediately, even when that involves eating some really gross fish.

For this reason, this book was created—for the glory of Jesus. The reality is that there are 2.5 million mosques around the world each denying the deity of Christ five times every day. This means that Christ's deity is denied 12.5 million times each day. My goal must be to lift Jesus up continually. I pray this book encourages others to do the same among Muslims.

- PART ONE -

Sharing with Muslims

"Every Christian is either a missionary or an imposter."
Charles Spurgeon

For many, the thought of sharing the gospel with Muslims is daunting at best. And yet, there is the mandate to "Go...and make disciples of all nations" (Matt. 28:19). Surely that includes people who are part of the second largest religion in the world. The Lord desires every one of the almost two billion Muslims to be in relationship with Him. The question then becomes, how do we share the gospel with Muslims? What does this look like? Where do we start, and what is the end goal?

This guide presents thirteen topics designed to help guide you through the ins and outs of sharing the gospel with Muslims and discipling them. For this guide to be an effective tool, two presumptions have been made. First, you are a committed follower of Jesus and have a desire to see all people groups worship the Lord in Spirit and in truth. Second, you have a desire to see Muslims reached for Jesus.

For this study, you will need to find a partner in Jesus with whom to work. Jesus sent the twelve and then the seventy-two out in pairs, and it is true that we are better together.[1] Although you might have some fruit on your own, by working with a partner your growth will be exponential. Your faith will be elevated as you pray together to see your Muslim friends come to faith in Jesus. Your prayers will be more powerful as you join in unity. Your testimony will be more credible as the two of you share of your love for Jesus. But be forewarned, more than two can be a bit overwhelming for your new Muslim friend. He or she might feel a bit overwhelmed by your enthusiasm.

Let this manual serve as a resource for you as you seek to share the truth of Jesus with your Muslim friend. It is but one way of sharing the gospel and discipling and certainly not on par with the Scriptures. It is meant to be used as a tool and shared. Upon completion of this manual with a friend, I recommend that each of you find a new friend to model sharing the gospel with Muslims. In this way, more Muslims are hearing the gospel and seeing the love of Jesus.

CHAPTER 1

Know Their Content and Then Know Their Story

> "Evangelism is just one beggar telling another beggar where to find bread."
>
> *D. T. Niles*

In order to share the gospel effectively, we must understand the context in which we are ministering. In this case, the context is the lives and culture of Muslims. Before anything can be done, we must first understand the background of Muslims and their religion. Understanding Islam is a daunting task. There are so many facets and pieces that no two people understand Islam in the same way. That being said, the basics of Islam are things that everyone should know before engaging a Muslim in a conversation of eternal significance. Thus, we will begin with basic information about Islam.

THE BASICS OF ISLAM

The religion of Islam has two main components: *iman* (beliefs) and *deen* (duties). The following illustration represents these components in an easy-to-understand format. The *deen* (duties/pillars) are the legs and the *iman* (beliefs) set on the top (see Figure 1), illustrating that the duties a Muslim performs holds up his faith.

FIGURE 1: *Islam's Beliefs and Duties*

IMAN *(Beliefs)*		
ALLAH (Prophets)	ANGELS (Last Days)	BOOKS (Decrees)
SHAHADA · SALAT	ZAKAT · SOWM	HAJJ · JIHAD
DEEN *(Duties/Pillars)*		

IMAN (Beliefs)

- **ALLAH**

The Arabic word for God is *Allah*. Whether you're a Christian, a Jew, an atheist, or a Muslim, if you speak Arabic, you will use the word *Allah* when referring to God.

For Muslims, Allah surpasses all human knowledge. He is transcendent and non-personal and, therefore, cannot be known. For the Muslim, belief in Allah involves an intellectual acceptance, verbal confession, and appropriate action in accordance with the commands of Islam.

Tawhid is the foundational characteristic of Allah and encompasses the idea of the oneness of God. Muslims are strict monotheists and have no place for any plurality within the Godhead (i.e., the Trinity). Muslims see Christians as worshipping three separate gods which constitutes the greatest sin. The Quran is divided into chapters, or *sura* in Arabic. In Surah 1:12 of the Quran, it says, "Say, He is Allah, the One and Only Allah, the Eternal, the Absolute, He begetteth not, nor is He begotten; And there is none like unto Him." It is important to understand the significance of tawhid. Christians often say they agree with the primary part of the Muslim creed: "There is no God but God." However, the concept of tawhid to a Muslim is that not only is there one God but that there is no such thing as a Triune God. In essence, tawhid denies Jesus as the Son of God.

- **ANGELS**

Angels occupy a prominent place in the Quran and are placed above the messengers, or prophets. They are also sanctified from carnal desires and never disobey Allah. This means they can never commit sin. However, in Quran 2:30, angels argue with Allah that he should not create Adam.

Among the host of angels, four take precedence:

- Jibril (Gabriel) is the angel of revelation (Quran 2:97–98). Other names and titles are given to Gabriel in the Quran such as the "faithful spirit" and the "holy spirit" (Quran 16:102).
- Mikail (Michael) is the angel of sustenance.

- Israfil is the angel who will blow the trumpet at the end of the world.
- Izra'il is the angel of death. Although there are no references to him in the Quran, there are references to Izra'il in the *hadith* (traditions).

There are seven activities that angels perform according to the Quran:

1. Angels write mankind's deeds: "Behold two angels appointed to learn his doings, learn and note them, one sitting on the right and one on the left. Not a word does he utter but there is a sentinel by him, ready to note it" (Quran 50:17–18).
2. Angels receive sinners and punish them: "Thou couldst see, when the angels take the souls of unbelievers at death; how they smite their faces and their backs saying, 'Taste the penalty of the blazing fire'" (Quran 8:50).
3. Angels implore forgiveness for those who believe: "Those who sustain the throne of God and those around it sing glory and praise to their Lord; believe in Him; and implore forgiveness for those who believe" (Quran 40:7).
4. Angels are the guardians of hell: "And we have set none but angels as guardians of the fire; and we have fixed their number" (Quran 74:31).
5. Angels are Allah's messengers: "Praise be to Allah, who created out of nothing the heavens and the earth, who made the angels messengers with wings" (Quran 35:1).
6. Angels praise Allah: "And thou wilt see the angels surround the throne on all sides, singing glory and praise to their Lord" (Quran 39:75).
7. Angels carry Allah's throne: "And the angels be on its sides, and eight will, that day, bear the throne of thy Lord above them" (Quran 69:17).

In addition to angels, who are perfect, sinless beings, there are *jinn*, who are created spiritual beings that can be good or evil. According to the Quran, jinn were created from smokeless fire.[1] According to the hadith, jinn can marry, have children, and die. Although they are invisible, they can appear to people in various forms. Like mankind, the jinn are in need of salvation. In Quran 72:1–2, 11–15, some jinn believed Mohammad as the last messenger of Allah and became Muslims. Therefore, they will enter into paradise, while unbelieving jinn will be condemned to hell.

- **BOOKS OF ALLAH**

For Muslims, all the sacred, revealed books have one source: the eternal tablet (Quran 55:15). This eternal tablet is the heavenly archetype of Scripture. From it, material was revealed through the angel Gabriel to the prophets at various times throughout history (Quran 13:38). This revelation happens through the process of *tanzil*, or bringing down, of the message from paradise to earth. Tradition says the eternal tablet rests in Allah's presence and is located directly above the *Kaaba*,[2] which is considered the center of the earth.

According to the hadith, one hundred four books have been revealed to mankind through the prophets. These include:

- Adam: 10 books
- Seth: 50 books
- Enoch: 30 books
- Abraham: 10 books
- Moses: One book (Torah/*Tawrat*)[3]
- David: One book (Psalms/*Zabur*)[4]
- Jesus: One book (Gospel/*Injil*)[5]
- Mohammad: One book (Quran)

Many of these books have been lost and so cannot be read or studied.

- **PROPHETS OF ALLAH**

According to the hadith, Allah sent 124,000 prophets/messengers.[6] We will note some of the more important prophets and their names used in the Quran. It is important to know the names of these prophets so that when you refer to them, your Muslim friend will know of whom you are speaking. It is also vital to realize that the narratives and teachings of many biblical characters in the Quran do not match the biblical accounts (see Table 1). This means that although you might refer to the story of Joseph to illustrate a point, the Muslim will know a different story and may not understand the point you are trying to make. It is for this reason it is best to simply tell the biblical stories as they are written (or better yet, allow the Muslim to read the story from the Bible himself) before discussing any potential applications or points.

TABLE 1: *The Names of Prophets*

QURANIC NAME	BIBLICAL NAME
Adam	Adam
Idris	Enoch
Nuh	Noah
Ibrahim	Abraham
Lut	Lot
Ayuub	Job
Ishaq	Isaac
Ismail	Ishmael
Yaqub	Jacob
Yusuf	Joseph
Musa	Moses
Harrun	Aaron
Dawud	David
Sulaiman	Solomon
Elia	Elijah
Alyasa	Elisha
Yunus	Jonah
Dhulkitel	Ezekiel
Zakariya	Zachariah
Yahya	John the Baptist
Isa	Jesus

Muslims revere Mohammad as the final messenger of Allah. He is given the place of highest honor and respect. Because of his high position, Muslims never utter the name of Mohammed without following it by saying, "The prayers of Allah be upon him." He is described as *rasul* (messenger), *nabi Allah* (prophet of Allah), and *khatim al-anbia* (the seal of the prophets) in Quran 33:40. Followers of Islam believe there will never be more prophets or messengers after Mohammad because the final revelation from Allah came through him. In fact, Muslims believe that all the prophets were Muslims, even if they never referred to themselves as such (Quran 3:67).

- **THE LAST DAYS**

Of particular importance to Muslims is the "Day of Judgment," also known as "The Hour" in the Quran. This moment is one of the principle themes of Quranic teaching and is closely connected with the resurrection of the dead when everyone will rise to be judged. According to the Quran, no one knows the hour of this special day except Allah. The return of Jesus Christ is the firm sign of the approach of the Day of Judgment (Quran 43:60–61). The hadith expounds on this idea of Jesus' return by stating that Jesus will kill the Antichrist and rule the earth for forty years. He will kill all the swine, forbid the eating of pork, marry and have children, preach Islam, destroy the cross, defeat the Jews, and destroy unrepentant Christians (i.e., those Christians who are unwilling to submit to Islam). Jesus will then die and be buried in Medina, next to the grave of Mohammad, and rise again on judgment day.

Judgment day is said to be like one thousand years (Quran 22:47). The place of judgment is unknown, though it is believed to be somewhere on earth. During that time, there will be a "weighing of the deeds" (Quran 42:17; 55:7-9; 57:25) where good deeds and bad deeds of individuals will be placed on giant scales and judged. Their judgment could include a time in hell. Hell is seen as a temporary time of schooling for bad Muslims and a place for unbelieving jinn and people to reside for eternity (Quran 7:179; 32:13, 14; 90:1–10). Paradise, on the other hand, is the place where all Muslims strive to go after death. It is said to be full of beautiful women, rivers of alcohol, honey, and milk, all kinds of halal (allowed) meat, various fruits, and beautiful palaces, clothes, and unending sensual pleasures (Quran

43:68–73; 47:15; 52:17-28; 55:46-78; 56:8–38). It is important to note that nowhere in the Quran or the hadith is there any mention of being with God for all of eternity. It seems paradise is a reward of all those things that had previously been forbidden.

- **PREDESTINATION (DECREES)**

Simply stated, the teaching of the Quran is that Allah decrees everything. Nothing can put any restrictions on the timeless plans of his decrees. He bestows bounty on whom he will (Quran 3:73–74) and he exalts whom he will (Quran 3:26). Allah sends whom he will astray and guides whom he will.[7] Everything has been created according to his fixed decrees. However, because Allah is unknowable, so is his will. Allah is not bound by any covenants made with his creation. Revelation, then, is not to make Allah known, but rather to give mankind a set of guidelines to follow. Thus, this means Muslims must submit to the revelation and to the inevitable. There is a teaching in the Quran that Allah has decided and determined all that has taken place and all that will happen (Quran 6:59; 17:13; 22:70). This has created a culture of fatalism where mankind has no control over anything. This is seen when a Muslim, who smokes multiple packs of cigarettes a day, is not worried by the possibility of lung cancer or emphysema because if Allah wills him to be sick, he will be sick and if Allah wills him not to be sick, he will not be sick. His behaviors hold no importance in this matter.

DEEN *(Duties/Pillars)*

- **SHAHADA – *The Declaration of Faith***

Shahada literally means "testimony" and is the Muslim profession of faith. It consists of two sentences:

1. *La ilaha ila allah* ("There is no deity except Allah"): Although it seems that we, as monotheistic Christians should agree with this statement, we do not. The concept here is that of tawhid, or the oneness of God. In this statement is a declaration against the Trinity and, therefore, a denial of the deity of Christ. We believe in the Triune

God: Father, Son, and Holy Spirit. This belief is considered *shirk* (blasphemy) by Muslims. Thus, we cannot say that we agree with this part of the shahada. To do so is denying the deity of Christ, which for us is blasphemy.
2. *Wa Mohammad rasul Allah* ("And Mohammad is the messenger of Allah"): Every Christian would agree that we do not agree with this statement. We do not hold to the fact that Mohammad is the final messenger of Allah. To do so is to negate Jesus' authority.

- **SALAT – *Prayer***

Salit or prayer is at the heart of Islam and the Muslim's way of life (Quran 2:186). There is a beautiful devotion to remembering Allah throughout the day that we, as Christians, can and should respect. What would happen if we stopped five times a day to turn our hearts and faces toward God and simply basked in His presence? It's a beautiful and challenging idea.

Muslims believe there are five times of prayer that were prescribed when Mohammad ascended into paradise for a glimpse of the afterlife. These times of prayer that are dictated by the sun include:

1. *Fijr:* At dawn before sunrise
2. *Dhuhr:* Just after midday, after the sun passes its zenith
3. *Asr:* In the late afternoon
4. *Maghrib:* Immediately after sunset
5. *Isha:* After sunset and before midnight

Prayers can be said anywhere provided the Muslim is not ceremonially unclean, such as when a woman is on her monthly cycle, nor the place considered unclean, such as a bathroom. Extra merit is given to men who perform their prayers in public. The position of the prayer must be towards the *qibla*, which is the direction of Mecca, or, more precisely, toward the black stone, a meteorite built into the western corner of the Kaaba. When Muslims pray outside the mosque, they use a prayer mat to separate them from the world. Women must pray in their houses, or separately from men if they are in a mosque.

For the prayer to be considered valid, a precise pattern of actions and recited Arabic words must be followed. It involves standing, bowing, kneeling, prostrating, and sitting. This round of actions must be performed a set number of times at each time of prayer (for example, twice at dawn). So during the five times of compulsory prayer, seventeen rounds are performed each day.

Prayer is always preceded by ritual washing, or ablutions. This is to cleanse parts of the body prior to praying to Allah. These ablutions must be performed in the correct order or the prayer will be considered invalid. In the absence of water, the person praying can use sand.

- **ZAKAT –** *Almsgiving*

Zakat is derived from the root word *zaka*, which means "to be pure," and means the purification of increase of one's possessions. Just as the ablutions purify the person's body before going to prayer, zakat purifies the person's possessions. Zakat is part of a Muslim's earnings, plus part of his savings, given as a compulsory payment in the name of Allah. Zakat is paid once a year and works out to be approximately 2.5 percent of a person's income. It is prescribed by the Quran as a form of piety for all believers (Quran 2:43, 110, 117, 277; 9:5). However, the system of determining and collecting zakat varies from country to country, between the differing sects of Islam, and from family to family.

- **SOWM –** *Fasting During Ramadan*

The origin of Muslim fasting is likely from the practice of fasting by Jews and Christians. "O ye who believe! Fasting is prescribed to you as it was prescribed to those before you" (Quran 2:183). Fasting is obligatory for all Muslims, male and female, who are adult and of sound mind and body. Fasting is not obligatory for those who are sick, traveling, women on their monthly cycle, nor women who are pregnant or nursing. Missed fasts should be made up. If that is not possible, the freeing of a slave, feeding the poor, or giving alms or other charitable works can be substituted for the fast.

Muslims fast from sunrise to sunset during the holy month of Ramadan. In Islamic understanding, to fast means not eating, drinking, swallowing saliva, or having sexual intercourse from the moment the light of true dawn appears until the time the sun disappears below the horizon at sunset.

- HAJJ – *Pilgrimage to Mecca*

The *hajj* is the world's largest religious gathering each year. Approximately two million Muslims descend upon Mecca in Saudi Arabia annually for this event. The pilgrimage is actually a combination of two pilgrimages: the *umra*, which was originally performed in the spring, and the hajj, which was performed in the autumn. The umra is centered on Mecca, while the hajj is centered on Arafat, a vast plain about twelve miles from Mecca. The two pilgrimages have been combined into one and are now referred to simply as hajj.

The umra consists of two ceremonies which take place in Mecca. The first, *tawaf*, is the circumambulation of the Kaaba which is performed seven times. At the beginning of each circuit, the pilgrim touches or kisses the black stone. The second, *sa'y*, is the time of running. The Muslim must run between *as'Saja* and *al-Marwa*, two small hills where the two most important idols of pre-Islamic Arabia resided. The pilgrim must run between them seven times.

According to the Quran and hadith, the Kaaba was originally built by Adam, destroyed in the flood of Noah, and then rebuilt by Abraham and Ishmael. The nearby well of Zamzam is said to have miraculously appeared when Hagar was looking frantically for water to quench Ishmael's thirst after she was sent away by Abraham.

The second pilgrimage, the hajj, lasts six days during a particular time of the year. It begins with an address at the mosque and midday prayers. Pilgrims then leave Mecca for Arafat. Muslims must arrive at Arafat by noon on the designated day. From just after midday until sunset, pilgrims stand before Allah in the plain of Arafat. This standing is the most important part of the hajj. If a pilgrim misses even part of it, his hajj is invalid. They then make their way to Mina where the pilgrims collect seventy small stones. At Mina there are three pillars: the first, the middle, and the steep one. Each pilgrim throws his stones at the steep one which is seen as a symbol of stoning Satan. Pilgrims are then to provide an animal sacrifice since this place is believed to be the place where Abraham was willing to sacrifice his son. After this, the pilgrim's head is shaved, he returns to Mecca to circumambulate the Kaaba and has a joyous time of shopping, eating, and socializing.

According to the hadith, a pilgrim who performs the pilgrimage sincerely and with the right intentions comes out like a new baby, born fresh and sinless to start life anew. In other words, all the individual's sins have been removed. This is not to say those sins have been atoned for. There is no atonement. It is a removal of any previous sins.

- **JIHAD – *Struggle***

Although non-Muslims hear of *jihad* in connection with holy war or the use of force, the word jihad carries a number of meanings for the Muslim. It expresses the personal struggle against evil in one's life and a determination to overcome it and to do good. There is the jihad of the pen or tongue when one is trying to convert unbelievers to Islam or working to improve the moral framework of Islamic society through speaking and writing. These forms are called the "greater jihad." The jihad which uses arms and force is called the "lesser jihad."[8]

Application

1. What is your major takeaway after learning about Islam through the reading and through the above teaching?
2. With your partner, find a Muslim who is open to sharing about their faith. Be sure to ask them about how they pray, about paradise and hell, their thoughts on Islam and about God. You may also want to ask about their culture, family, and other areas that will help you understand their context more fully. Do not try to debate any points related to Islam. Simply use this as a time to get to know them. Show yourself as a good listener and learner.

CHAPTER 2

Start with a Divine Mandate

> "Evangelism is the spontaneous overflow of a glad and free heart in Jesus Christ."
>
> *Robert Munger*

DIVINE APPOINTMENTS

"And he had to pass through Samaria."

John 4:4

In the first three verses of John 4, we learn that Jesus is having a bit of trouble with Jewish religious leaders in Jerusalem. So He leaves and goes to Galilee to continue His ministry. On the way, He travels through Samaria. This is significant because Jews despised Samaritans. In fact, most Jews took a much longer route from Judea to Galilee just to avoid it. But Jesus takes the "road less traveled" and walks right through this town.

There are two important points regarding Jesus' trek through Samaria. First, Jesus leaves Judea for strategic reasons. The religious leaders are upset with Him and so rather than inciting them further, Jesus chooses to leave knowing the time of His arrest and crucifixion have not yet arrived. Sometimes our lives take twists and turns simply because of extenuating circumstances. The religious leaders are upset with Jesus so He chooses to leave. On one hand this seems like a very un-spiritual way of making a decision. However, the Lord uses our circumstances to bring us to places where His gospel can be preached. Sometimes the most spiritual thing you can do is submit to your leader and move to a new place or realize that the delay in your day might be divinely inspired. Do not despise circumstantial changes or moves. Sometimes these open doors you never thought possible.

The second point is to be led by the Spirit. John 4:4 tells us that Jesus "had to" go through Samaria. This is not actually accurate. He could go around Samaria. It would take Him much longer, but He would get to Galilee. This tells us that there is something deeper at work. Jesus has to go through Samaria not because of His situation or surroundings but because of a divine urging. Jesus knows He was to meet a very special woman. He is intentional. We must be led by the Spirit in the same way. There is no substitution for knowing the voice of the Spirit and then obeying immediately. The Lord delights in using us for His glory. We must learn to know His voice by spending extravagant time with Jesus and abiding in Him.

GETTING CONNECTED

Mike Shipman, the author of the book *Any-3: Anyone, Anywhere, Any Time*,[1] writes that we should share the gospel with anyone at any time in any place. There are no qualifiers to the Great Commission. It does not say go into all the world except where it's difficult. No, it simply tells believers to go and preach. Jesus went to and shared the gospel with a despised people. They were difficult. They were the enemy. They needed the truth.

There are five steps to the Any-3 method:

1. Get connected.
2. Get to God.
3. Get to lostness.
4. Get to the gospel.
5. Get to a decision.

In this chapter, we are looking at the first step of the Any-3 method: getting connected. The first part of getting connected is to find places where Muslims hang out in your community. It isn't rocket science. It's simply observation. This is the strategic part. Jesus leaves Judea for strategic reasons. In the same way, putting yourself where Muslims congregate is for strategic reasons. Essentially, the more Muslims with whom you are in regular interaction through daily life, the more opportunities you will have to share the gospel of Jesus with them.

The second part of being connected is to be completely led by the Holy Spirit. This involves abiding in Jesus and being willing to be led into the unknown. There are ways that we can cultivate hearing the voice of the Holy Spirit. First, you should expect the Holy Spirit to speak to you and through you as He did to the early Christians in the book of Acts (8:39; 10:19–20). Second, spend time in the Word expecting the Holy Spirit to speak to you personally through what you are reading. Third, talk to God every day. Be sure that you are taking time to listen for the voice of the Spirit as He speaks to you. Fourth, pray daily in your heavenly language. This will help you become more sensitive to His voice. Fifth, expect the gifts of the Holy Spirit to be manifested through you. This might include things like a word of knowledge for someone or the gift of healing. The actual gift itself is not significant, but the glory of God is. Sixth, listen for and expect God to speak to you through others. Seventh, be willing to take a risk, even if it might mean you fail. There are times we are sure of the voice of God and it is true and we celebrate. There are other times we are sure of the voice of God and it is not true. Just as a baby learning to walk stumbles and occasionally falls, we learn by trying over and over.

Once you've completed the essential parts of getting connected, there must be follow up. A simple way of keeping track of all your connections is through an evangelism journal (see Appendix A). To be effective, start by filling in any background information. This will include the person's name, where you met, what time, a physical description (since many Muslims have the same name), and then what you talked about as well as any prayer requests your connection may have. Then fill out what happens in each subsequent meeting. Do this as soon as your meeting is over so it is still fresh in your mind. This journal will serve as your guide to praying effectively for the Muslims with whom you are in connection. It also serves as a guide as you prayerfully discern where God is leading your conversation. There is no perfect way of sharing the gospel. There is no silver bullet that brings all Muslims immediately to Christ. Each person is an individual and the Lord will meet her where she is. But you must be led by the Spirit to discern the next step. Maybe God wants you to tell her a particular Bible story or use a resource available in her heart language. Jot down what you feel the Lord is saying so you will remember before meeting with her again.

Additionally, utilize the Evangelism Tracking Chart (see Appendix B). Put each new contact on the sheet, and meet with your partner regularly to discuss where each contact is on the chart. This will help you see how they are progressing on their journey of finding Christ. It will also help indicate when they are ready to begin meeting in a local fellowship.

Application

1. What is your biggest takeaway from this chapter? What challenges you? What excites you? What scares you? Share this with your partner.
2. Have you ever felt a divine urging? If so, what happened?
3. With your partner, write down all the places you can think of where Muslims hang out.
4. Together, choose a place and time to visit one or more of the places on your list. When you visit, be sure to engage Muslims in conversation by simply asking them about themselves. Take time to get acquainted with them: who they are, their family, their work, their hobbies, the topics are not crucial. Simply be friendly and open to the work of the Holy Spirit.
5. When your visit is finished, take time with your partner to pray for your new friend. Then fill in an evangelism journal entry for her/him.

CHAPTER 3

Engage in Intentional Interaction

"The salvation of a single soul is more important than the production or preservation of all the epics and tragedies in the world."

C. S. Lewis

BE INTENTIONALLY OBEDIENT

"So he came to a town of Samaria called Sychar, near the field that Jacob had given to his son Joseph. Jacob's well was there; so Jesus, wearied as he was from his journey, was sitting beside the well. It was about the sixth hour."

John 4:5–6

On this occasion, Jesus witnesses sitting beside a well. He isn't at a synagogue. He isn't in the Temple. In fact, most of Jesus' witnessing experiences throughout the gospels occur in the course of everyday life. In the same way, most of our witnessing opportunities occur in everyday life. This is because the gospel becomes more relevant when presented within the context of day-to-day living. In this way, the witnessing encounter doesn't feel "staged" and the person doesn't feel "set up." Moreover, when we are open to the leading of the Holy Spirit, He creates opportunities in the mundane that can be used for His glory to shine. That is why we must be intentional about our days. This means every morning we lay our day at the foot of the cross. We have plans and ideas of what the day may bring, but by giving all of that to Jesus, He is able to take our meager, finite plans and create something of divine significance.

A great example of this is in John 2:1–11 where Jesus performs His first miracle: turning water into wine at the wedding in Cana. For me, it is not the act of Jesus turning the water into wine that is the most significant part of this story, but verses 6 to 8 that hold the most substance. "Now there were six stone water jars there for the Jewish rites of purification, each holding twenty or thirty gallons. Jesus said to the servants, 'Fill the jars with water.' And they filled them up to the brim. And he said to them, 'Now draw some out and take it to the master of the feast.' So they took it" (John 2:6–8).

Filling thirty-gallon stone jars with water is a mundane task. It is something the servants do all the time. Here they are at the wedding, probably with many tasks to complete, and Jesus asks them to fill the stone jars. Our twenty-first century minds easily gloss this over. However, in the days of Jesus, there were no faucets or hoses to use. There were only servants with smaller jars going to the well, filling them with water, carrying them back to the larger jars, and pouring the water in. The servants go back and forth from the well to the stone jars, obeying the seemingly mundane command of Jesus. I'm sure there is quite a bit of mumbling among the servants as they trek back and forth with their heavy loads. The result? These servants have a front-row seat to Jesus' first miracle. Jesus uses their mundane task for His glory. The lowest members of society see Jesus perform the miraculous. Similarly, we must ask God to take our mundane tasks and use them for His glory.

In order for this to work, you must be willing to leave your comfort zone. Samaria is not a naturally comfortable place for Jesus. Samaritans despise Jews and Jews hate Samaritans. Even so, Jesus leaves the comforts of the known at the urging of the Spirit of God. In the same way, we must leave our comfort zones behind and be willing to die to self. This will mean interruptions. This will mean being uncomfortable. This will mean relinquishing control. But this will also mean a front-row seat to the miraculous.

This is more than just a method for reaching Muslims. This is a lifestyle. It is a lifestyle of surrender. It is a lifestyle that says, "He must increase, but I must decrease" (John 3:30). It is a lifestyle that reaches across human boundaries with the love of Christ for the glory of God.

Application

1. What is your takeaway from this chapter? How did it challenge you?
2. Has Jesus done the miraculous through your mundane before? If so, share this with your partner.
3. If you were successful in meeting at least one Muslim from the previous chapter's application, return to that place with your partner and connect with another woman or man. If not, look at your list of possible locations from the previous chapter and choose a different location to visit with your partner.
4. Again, take time with your partner to pray for any Muslim you encounter. Then fill in an evangelism journal entry for any new Muslims you meet.
5. Choose a time and place to get together with your partner to pray over all your evangelism journal entries. Commit to praying for them every day.

CHAPTER 4

Relinquish Your Power and Embrace Your Need

"The history of missions is the history of answered prayer. It is the key to the whole mission problem. All human means are secondary."

Samuel Zwemer

SHOW A REAL NEED FOR OTHERS

*"A woman from Samaria came to draw water.
Jesus said to her, 'Give me a drink.'"*

John 4:7

You cannot help but notice the interactive, conversational tone of Jesus as He shares with the Samaritan woman. Jesus initiates the conversation by requesting a drink, then the Samaritan woman responds. He has a need: He is thirsty. In asking her for a drink, He places Himself below her. The God of all creation humbles Himself to be in a place of need so that the truth of His gospel can be revealed. The Greek from this passage implies a request that, in English, requires the word "please." He asks and she has a choice. She can choose to say no and walk away or she can choose to say yes and provide this Jewish man with the water He needs.

Similarly, we must choose to live in community with Muslims. Muslims are a truly communal people. It's a tenet of their faith called *ummah*. The idea of ummah is that everyone works together for the common good of all and the expansion of Islam. Everything is done together. It is why a young woman agrees to marry a man she has never met, knowing that by doing so she is helping her family through her future husband's connections, finances, or occupation. By intentionally working to learn their language, live the way they live, and dress in a way that is respectful to them, we can join the community and become an integral part. As we live in community, there will be moments when we are in need. Someone from our local Muslim community can then answer that need. Something as commonplace as a recommendation on where to buy good pita bread shows respect and honor for your Muslim friend. Just like Jesus placed Himself under the Samaritan woman when He asked her for a drink, when we ask members of the local Muslim community for help, we elevate them over us, showing them we need them. It is honoring. It opens the door for the gospel. The easy way is to look it up online or figure it out on your own. But by choosing to relinquish your power and embrace your need, you develop a deeper place within the community.

Application

1. With your partner, discuss ways to be a part of your local Muslim community. For example, baking cookies for neighbors, visiting with shopkeepers, or meeting people at a local café.
2. In our passage in John 4, we see the Samaritan woman as a person of peace.[1] She was receptive to the message and took it to others. With your partner, brainstorm anyone in your community who might be a person of peace. If no one comes to mind, brainstorm places you might go to find a person of peace.
3. Commit to a time of prayer with your partner over your evangelism journal entries.
4. Prayerfully follow up with your contacts through another meeting. Before meeting, think of something you need and then ask your contact for help. Be sure to fill out the evangelism journal for any meetings you may have.

CHAPTER 5

Take Risks to Reach Out

"Say 'no' to self and 'yes' to Jesus every time."
William Borden

THE RISK OF TRUST

"The Samaritan woman said to him, 'How is it that you, a Jew, ask for a drink from me, a woman of Samaria?' (For Jews have no dealings with Samaritans)."

John 4:9

Trusting someone is hard; especially if you don't know that person well. In John 4:9, we see the Samaritan woman struggles with trusting Jesus. She sees Him as the enemy. He's a Jew, she's a Samaritan. There is no real reason for Him to talk with her. There is no reason for her to trust Him. However, as Jesus put Himself in a place of humility by asking her for a drink, her defenses are lowered. This opens the door for her to begin to trust Him. But for this simple act she would never have spoken to Him. And speaking to Him opens the door for a life change.

In much the same way, we must first take the risk of trusting the local people. We may not be enemies like the Jews and the Samaritans, but there certainly are cultural differences that make trust difficult. When we open our hearts and choose to trust our local community to help when we need it, it paves the way for them to begin to trust us. Through that carefully-cultivated trust, our neighbors will be able to hear and respond to the message of Christ.

Application

1. Is there anyone in your local community you trust? How did that trust develop?
2. How did your Muslim friend respond to your request or need in the last meeting? Discuss with your partner how you might facilitate a deeper connection with your contacts.
3. Commit to a time of prayer with your partner over your contacts. Commit to daily prayer for them as well.
4. Follow up with your Muslim contacts. You may want to use the theme of trust in your next meeting by asking them what they think trust is and what makes a person trustworthy. Be sure to fill out your evangelism journal and add any new names to the evangelism tracking sheet.

CHAPTER 6

Develop Reciprocity and Interdependence

> "We must be global Christians with a global vision because our God is a global God."
>
> *John R. W. Stott*

THEY HAVE SOMETHING TO OFFER US

"Jesus answered her, 'If you knew the gift of God, and who it is that is saying to you, "Give me a drink," you would have asked him, and he would have given you living water.' The woman said to him, 'Sir, you have nothing to draw water with, and the well is deep. Where do you get that living water? Are you greater than our father Jacob? He gave us the well and drank from it himself, as did his sons and his livestock.'"

John 4:10–12

As bearers of the gospel, it is easy to see ourselves as the answer to the great need felt in the hearts of Muslims. However, Jesus is that answer and not us. We are merely the vessels He chooses to use. But not always. Sometimes He uses a donkey (Num. 22:21–39). Sometimes He speaks for Himself (Acts 9:1–19). So lest we think of ourselves higher than we should, it is important to remember that God is God and we are not. We are mortal, finite, needy human beings who just happen to know the answer to life's greatest question through God's unending grace: How do we find God?

In the John 4 passage, Jesus asks the Samaritan woman for a drink. She has access to something Jesus needs. We developed this idea in an earlier chapter. Jesus also has something the woman needs; and that is the living water of the Holy Spirit. Interestingly, she does not even realize she has this need in her heart. In showing her this need in her life, He develops interdependence. He needs her for the water, and she needs Him for the living water. He honors her by asking her to meet His need. He honors her by lovingly showing her what she truly needs.

The same is true for our Muslim friends. There is a void in their life they do not recognize. As we show them our needs and ask for help, we position ourselves in a humble place whereby we can honor them. As we honor them, we are then able to develop reciprocity—an interdependence that can and should lead to a conversation concerning their need for the Savior.

Jesus does have a unique advantage here. He is the Son of God. As the Son of God, He knows the Samaritan woman and speaks in a way that penetrates her heart. We do not share that privilege. But we do have the Holy Spirit. As we listen carefully for His voice, He may give us knowledge about those to whom we minister. He also may not. Whether or not words of knowledge come, we are still the vessel the Lord uses to share His truth with Muslims. We must be sensitive to the leading of the Holy Spirit and speak what and when He tells us and nothing more. He knows the hearts of our new friends. He knows what will bring them closer to Him.

GET TO GOD

Not only does Jesus initiate the conversation with the Samaritan woman, He takes the initiative to guide the conversation to its intended goal. Although not preachy or condescending, Jesus presents truth very directly and simply. He assumes the teacher role as the conversation progresses. However, He is never condescending or haughty. While maintaining an informal interactive teaching approach, Jesus becomes the authority. He asks pointed questions, guiding the conversation into spiritual truth and toward its ultimate goal of a decision for Christ.

We should emulate Jesus' approach. In building a rapport with people, we meet them on a personal level. We talk as equals. We develop reciprocity. As the conversation turns to spiritual matters, we take the initiative as teacher, while still using relaxed, interactive methodology. We must teach through exploratory questions and add personal input as necessary. We must rely on the guidance of the Holy Spirit as the conversation progresses.

The Samaritan woman becomes increasingly aware of who Jesus actually is as the witnessing conversation progresses. Her understanding increases from Jesus being a Jewish man (John 4:9) to being perhaps greater than Jacob (4:12) to being a prophet (4:19) to being the Messiah (4:25–26). Jesus' goal is to help the Samaritan woman understand that *He* is the promised

Savior. This is the goal of every significant conversation.

Today, the correct understanding of Jesus as Messiah is to understand that Jesus has already died to pay for our sin and shame, and that He has risen from the dead as proof that God received His sacrifice. This is the gospel that Jesus proclaimed after His resurrection (Luke 24:44–49). This is also the message preached by Paul and the Apostles (1 Cor. 15:1–4).

We are commissioned to share the gospel! The gospel is the primary message that we bring. Personal testimonies about peace and love, talk about Jesus' wisdom and power, and discussions from the holy books of other religions are at times beneficial.[1] However, only the gospel has power to save, and therefore should be the primary message shared. Be the bearer of the good news.

Application

1. Read 1 Corinthians 1:17–2:8 paying attention to references about the cross, the power of the gospel, and the way the gospel should be presented. Discuss the questions with your partner.
    - "For Christ did not send me to baptize but to preach the gospel, and not with words of eloquent wisdom, lest the cross of Christ be emptied of its power" (v. 17).
        - Do clever methods void the gospel of its power?
        - What does this mean for us as disciples of Christ who share the good news?
    - "For the word of the cross is folly to those who are perishing, but to us who are being saved it is the power of God" (v. 18).
        - How can we present the gospel in a way that it does not convince lost people of our intelligence but rather points to Jesus?
    - "But we preach Christ crucified, a stumbling block to Jews and folly to Gentiles, but to those who are called, both Jews and Greeks, Christ the power of God and the wisdom of God" (vv. 23–24).
        - Is the gospel message appropriate to be proclaimed to all people groups and religions?
        - What does it mean that Christ crucified is a stumbling block to Jews and folly for Gentiles? What might it be for Muslims?
    - "For consider your calling, brothers: not many of you were wise according to worldly standards, not many were powerful, not many were of noble birth" (v. 26).
        - Should we share the gospel with only the affluent or with all people?
        - What does this mean for us right now?
    - And I, when I came to you, brothers, did not come proclaiming to you the testimony of God with lofty speech or wisdom. For I decided to know nothing among you except Jesus Christ and him crucified" (vv. 1–2).
        - What is the one message which must be shared?

2. Commit to pray with your partner for your contacts. Discuss follow up with them as you look over your evangelism journal entries. Create a plan for contacting your contacts for the purpose of follow up.

CHAPTER 7

Go Beyond the Superficial

"The Gospel is only good news if it gets there in time."
Carl F. H. Henry

EXCHANGE THE SUPERFICIAL FOR THE REAL THING

"Jesus said to her, 'Everyone who drinks of this water will be thirsty again, but whoever drinks of the water that I will give him will never be thirsty again. The water that I will give him will become in him a spring of water welling up to eternal life.' The woman said to Him, 'Sir, give me this water, so that I will not be thirsty or have to come here to draw water.'

Jesus said to her, 'Go, call your husband, and come here.' The woman answered him, 'I have no husband.' Jesus said to her, 'You are right in saying, "I have no husband"; for you have had five husbands, and the one you now have is not your husband. What you have said is true.'"

John 4:13–18

This precious woman is simply at a well to draw water. She does not make the trek to the well for any purpose other than that. However, Jesus shines a light on her situation. And it is a situation she must have contemplated daily on her walk to the well. In so doing, she is ready to hear the truth Jesus proclaims. Then she is ready to accept the living water He offers. She comes to the well for regular water. She leaves the well with a heart full of the Spirit of God.

In the same way, as we converse with Muslims, we must remember that they are in the middle of their lives. The Lord wants to interrupt their mundane daily chores to show them His truth and to give them His living water. We, as the bearers of the gospel, must be sensitive to the Holy Spirit as He uses us to demonstrate His love and truth. He is about to interrupt their lives. Are you ready to guide these precious ones to Jesus' living water?

SPEAK TO THE SHAME

We generally read the John 4 passage as a sinful woman receiving forgiveness from Jesus, with the concept of guilt and sin being the focal point of the story. However, there is so much more to this story that our Western eyes simply do not see. It is likely this unnamed woman with multiple husbands and a seemingly promiscuous lifestyle is, in fact, shamed simply because she is unable to have children. In a culture that places supreme importance on having children, especially sons, barrenness is a solid ground for divorce (Deut. 24:1). Therefore, it is highly probable that men married her, discovered she could not bear children, and divorced her to marry more fertile women. This changes how you view her, doesn't it?

The fear of infertility is a real issue for Muslim women. In Islamic tradition, having children is the most important Muslim religious injunction. In fact, a bride's status is not ensured until she demonstrates her fertility. In addition to Islamic beliefs about the sacred nature of bearing children, children are highly valued for social prestige as well as for the potential for future economic and physical support. Women feel great shame if they are unable to bear a child. This is then compounded with the fact that a man can take another wife if he chooses because of her infertility.

In highlighting the shame endured by the Samaritan woman, Muslims are able to identify with her need for protection as well as her feelings of shame. However, Jesus speaks to this woman in spite of her shame, her gender, and her ethnicity. His speech is that of love and acceptance, not scorn and disdain. In so doing, He honors her. He bypasses all her guilt and speaks directly to the need in her heart: the need for honor. When she leaves Jesus, her heart is healed enough for her to approach the men in the town to tell them about Him. Jesus honors her and it gives her the boldness to speak the truth to others. The same can be true for Muslims as they are freed from their shame and brought into God's family in a place of honor.

GET TO THE LOSTNESS

After transitioning from earthly subjects to spiritual matters, you should attempt to reveal the general problem of all mankind. Jesus can easily tell the woman to get her friends, but instead He chooses to expose her sin and shame. Jesus reveals the heart of the woman's problem in order to reveal the cure. Jesus does not permit the woman to ignore her sin and shame problem or find the cure without facing the sinful facts which brought her spiritual thirst. The woman has to admit and face her sinfulness and shame in order to be cured of its consequences.

This is the point of the conversation where Jesus' experience obviously separates from our experiences. Jesus is the Messiah, the sinless Son of God. Therefore, Jesus can no longer be on common ground with the woman by the well. However, every other follower of Jesus since that time shares the common experience of sinfulness and shame.

We should not avoid the topic of sin and shame and the consequences, nor should we come across "holier than thou." Instead, we should gently convince our Muslim friends of the reality of humanity's sin and shame along with its personal manifestations. This is accomplished as we admit that we also are sinners and full of shame and that we have faced its devastating consequences. Usually, the friend agrees to the part about being a sinner or having shame. Oftentimes, she will begin to discuss personal sins. Discussing the issue of personal sinfulness actually allows us to build more commonality and empathy with her. Witnessing relationships usually see commonality in the sense of common interests which the two parties enjoy. However, the sense of commonality is strengthened when both parties admit to a common problem and its negative effects in their lives. Lostness must necessarily precede salvation. The common state of lostness between us and our friends generally allows the witness to share the good news as the way out.

Sin and shame are easily brought into a discussion by speaking of current events that demonstrate sinful and shameful behaviors. Thefts, murders, corruption, and religious hypocrisy can lead to agreement about humanity's sinful and shameful condition. By simply asking the person what he is doing to obtain the forgiveness of sins, then asking if his sins are forgiven yet will usually result in the realization that his attempts to atone for sin and shame aren't effective. At this point agreement is generally reached about the joint sinfulness and shame of mankind.

An illustration of this concept can help as well. The point of the illustration is that all people are sinners and full of shame, and no matter how great or small their sins, all people are separated from God. The illustration is as follows:

- "As Islamic law states, certain foods like pork aren't permissible to be eaten. Let's suppose that I offer to you a bowl of cooked pork. May you eat it or not?
- The person naturally responds, "No, I am not permitted to eat it."
- "Suppose I only place a small piece of pork in a bowl. Then I cover it up with rice and vegetables, so that it is no longer visible. Are you permitted to eat the contents of that bowl?"
- The correct answer is that he may not eat the contents of that bowl either.
- "Which bowl will you choose to eat?"
- The Muslim might wrestle with the idea but will ultimately conclude that neither bowl of food containing pork may be eaten since the amount of the forbidden food doesn't matter.

At this point, present the scenario of two shameful sinners, one with obvious sins like murder and adultery, and another shameful sinner with smaller, less-obvious sins, such as saying mean words to a classmate. Which person will be received by God into heaven upon his death? The answer is that neither will be received because they are both sinners and God is holy. If the person is open to more discussion, you may wish to delve into the Islamic idea of scales that weigh good deeds and bad deeds. Adam and Eve were dispelled from Eden for the shame that came upon them after they committed one sin. How can we, who sin every day and are completely full of shame, ever atone for our sins? The problem with the scales is that they measure the wrong thing. Rather than comparing our good deeds versus our bad, since our good deeds can never cover our shame, we must compare ourselves with Jesus Christ, the sinless one. We can never come close to Him.

Application

1. How has your opinion of the Samaritan woman changed after this chapter?
2. What is your definition of shame and honor? What does it look like played out in someone's life? How might this differ from the Muslims around you?
3. In your follow up with your contacts, ask them to explain the idea of shame and honor to you. Follow the leading of the Holy Spirit as you speak to the shame felt and the honor needed which can only be found in Jesus.
4. Find a time to pray with your partner over your contacts. Commit to pray for them daily as well.

CHAPTER 8

Be Authentic and Transparent in Worship

"When Christ calls a man, he bids him come and die."
Dietrich Bonhoeffer

TRUE WORSHIP

"The woman said to him, 'Sir, I perceive that you are a prophet. Our fathers worshiped on this mountain, but you say that in Jerusalem is the place where people ought to worship.' Jesus said to her, 'Woman, believe me, the hour is coming when neither on this mountain nor in Jerusalem will you worship the Father. You worship what you do not know; we worship what we know, for salvation is from the Jews. But the hour is coming, and is now here, when the true worshipers will worship the Father in spirit and truth, for the Father is seeking such people to worship him.'"

John 4:19–23

John Piper once said that the reason missions exists is because worship does not. Basically, he was saying that God deserves to be worshiped in every people group on earth. When that is not happening, God then sends His followers to that area to preach His gospel so that He may be worshiped. Think about eternity. We will not be sharing the gospel with others in heaven. Everyone already knows the story. Everyone already has a relationship with Jesus. Instead, we will worship the Lord for all of eternity. Worship is eternal. So as we worship today, we are not only glorifying God; we are training for our eternal occupation. In John 12:32, Jesus says that if He is lifted up, He will draw all men to Him. I think Jesus has two meanings in mind when He speaks these words. The first is obvious, the cross. When Jesus is lifted up on the cross, He makes a way to bring humanity close to Him. But I also think this means that as we lift Him up in our worship, outsiders are drawn in.

Let me illustrate His point with a story from my own life. I befriended a Muslim Arab woman and we discussed many spiritual things together. However, she was not yet convinced that God saw her because she was a woman. One day, she came to my house and before she knocked on my door she heard me playing my keyboard and worshiping the Lord. She did not understand what I was singing because I was worshiping in English, but the presence of the Lord touched her heart. When she entered my living room, she began to question me about the music I was singing. She had never experienced music that could touch her heart in such a way. She did not know that the overflow of my heart of love for Jesus could be expressed in such a way. My worship brought her closer to Jesus. It was not my intention. I was simply worshiping as I did most days because Jesus is worthy of my worship. Even so, the Lord used my worship to show my dear friend that Jesus delights in me and in her, and longs to fill her with overflowing joy.

Even if you are not a musician, this concept applies to you. Jesus is worthy of worship for all eternity. And He is our best friend. Simply sharing the truth of who Jesus is and expressing how much you love Him is worship. Speaking about His characteristics in your conversations brings Jesus worship. As your Muslim friends see your unending devotion to Jesus, they will be drawn to Him.

RELAX

When significant conversations happen in informal contexts, the tone of the conversation is very relaxed. In fact, the tone of the conversation should not get tense until the internal battle with truth begins. One of the greatest challenges in witnessing is to share with the same relaxed tone of voice and mannerisms as when talking about non-spiritual things. Even in the transition to eternal subjects, the conversation should remain informative and relaxed. Think of it like this: when you are talking about your best friend, you might get a bit animated, but your face, your tone, and your mannerisms all reflect that you are speaking of someone you know and love deeply. There is no tension, no nervousness. It is the easiest thing in the world to talk about how much you love your best friend. In the same way, we must speak about Jesus. After all, He is our best friend.

That being said, no one has ever come to true faith in Christ without an intense inner battle. It is at this point the Holy Spirit is drawing your friend to a commitment. Tension at this point in the conversation is vital. The key is for you not to introduce the tension through personal nervousness, needless arguments, or a preachy approach to sharing the gospel. That way when the Holy Spirit draws the person to salvation, the person will turn to you to help guide them to truth rather than turn away from a conflict.

Be careful not to argue. If legitimate questions arise, answer them. Better yet, point the person to the Bible and have them read an appropriate passage for themselves. But do not be argumentative. People are rarely won to Christ through persuasive arguments. However, they are often won to Christ through a simple, loving presentation of the gospel.

GET TO THE GOSPEL

Jesus quickly draws a distinction between the religious beliefs held by the woman at the well compared to the true way of salvation that He taught and brought. To accomplish this, He clarifies the different religious understandings of the Samaritans and Jews. Jesus finds some common ground, stresses the commonality, and then shows the truthful difference which can save the woman at the well. Jesus then departs from commonality to show the truthful difference between what the woman believes and what is true.

The Samaritans held that Mt. Gerazim was especially sacred. Abraham and Jacob had built altars in the general vicinity (Gen. 12:7; 33:20) and the people were blessed from this mountain (Deut. 11:29; 27:12). In the Samaritan scripture, Mt. Gerazim was the mountain upon which Moses had commanded an altar to be built instead of Mt. Ebal (Deut. 27:4–6). In addition, the Samaritans had built a temple on Mt. Gerazim, which the Jews destroyed. This escalated tension and hostilities between the two parties that existed through the time of Christ.

For the Jews, Jerusalem was the appointed place for temple worship. So from the woman's perspective, the point of difference between the two religions is the place of worship. Jesus doesn't back away from truth in order to save the relationship with the hearer at this point. Rather, He clearly states, "Salvation is from the Jews" (John 4:22). There is only one reliable source of truth to be followed, and that is the revealed Word of God through Moses.

After establishing the source of authority, Jesus clarifies the woman's misunderstanding about the important aspects of true worship. According to Jesus, the point is not where a person worships, but the way a person worships (spirit and truth). Next, the woman expresses her limited but hopeful knowledge about the coming Messiah. He clears up any confusion because "He will declare all things to us" (John 4:25).

After agreeing on the issue of mutual sinfulness, the objective when sharing with your Muslim friend becomes to find the solution. Get to the gospel. Where does salvation come from? Every religion presupposes that humanity must do something in order to repair a broken or imperfect relationship between God and man. That's why each religion has its own different, but very similar, way to repair the separation between God and man. In Islam, people are potentially saved through keeping the five pillars (Chapter 2). However, the Bible shows a different way. Salvation comes by grace, through faith in the sacrifice of Jesus Christ, who paid mankind's sin debt with His own blood (Eph. 2:8–9). For the Muslim to find Christ, this truth must be proclaimed in love.

Application

1. What has been your biggest takeaway in this teaching so far? How have you changed?
2. How might you incorporate worship in your conversations with your contacts?
3. What challenges you the most as it relates to sharing the gospel to Muslims? What scares you? What excites you? Pray about these with your partner.
4. During your follow-up meetings, ask your contacts about salvation and how to be saved. Ask them what they are saved from and what it means to be saved. Ask them about forgiveness and how they obtain forgiveness of their sins. Then share what the Bible says about salvation and forgiveness. Be prepared to show them several passages concerning this topic. Be sure to make notes of your meetings in your evangelism journal.

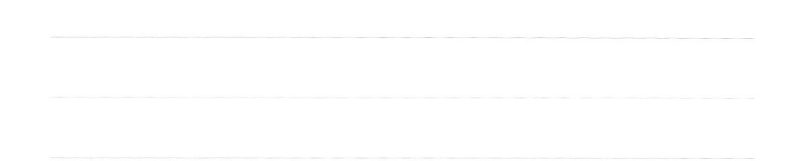

CHAPTER 9

Make a Life Changing Decision

"The Spirit of Christ is the spirit of missions.
The nearer we get to Him, the more intensely missionary we become."

Henry Martyn

GET TO A DECISION

"The woman said to him, 'I know that Messiah is coming (he who is called Christ). When he comes, he will tell us all things.' Jesus said to her, 'I who speak to you am he.'"

John 4:25–26

Had the woman not been open to Jesus' message, we assume that He would have heeded His own advice to His disciples. "And if any place will not receive you and they will not listen to you, when you leave, shake off the dust that is on your feet as a testimony against them" (Mark 6:11). But the woman is very open, and Jesus pursues follow up. He answers her questions and then declares Himself to be the Messiah. In the same way, as our Muslim friends open their hearts to the gospel, we must follow up regularly and speak boldly and clearly the truth of the gospel at every opportunity. Prayerfully discern which everyday activities might help you speak the truth of the gospel to your Muslim friend. Be intentional in the topics you bring up in conversation so that they may lead to eternal significance. Scripture is clear that we are not to be ashamed of the gospel but to proclaim it (Rom. 1:16; 2 Tim. 1:8; Phil. 1:20).

Application

1. Spend significant time in prayer with your partner concerning your contacts. Pray for their hearts to be open to the truth and for the Holy Spirit to make Himself known to them through dreams, visions, signs, and wonders. Commit to pray for your contacts daily.
2. During your follow-up time with your contacts, share the gospel again and bring the conversation to a point of decision. Ask each individual if they have any questions about what has been shared. Ask if they believe what you have told them. At this point, prayerfully decide to either ask them to make a decision or set a time to meet again.
   a. If your friend says that she/he believes what you have shared, have them read Romans 10:9–10. Explain that salvation comes through confessing Jesus as Lord and believing that Jesus died for her/his sins and shame and arose from the dead. Ideally, the new believer will want to invite her/his friends and family to discover this truth. Encourage her/him to prayerfully share the truth with those in her/his network. Then the fun of discipleship begins.
   b. If she/he is not yet ready to profess faith, prayerfully decide the next course of action. You may want to tell the Old Testament sacrifice stories of Adam and Eve, Cain and Abel, Noah, Abraham, and Moses. This will likely need to be in a future meeting time together. Encourage your Muslim friend to invite her/his friends and family to the meeting to hear and discuss the stories together.
3. Regardless of what happens, take some moments to thank the Lord with your partner. Thank Him for the privilege of sharing His truth.
4. Be sure to fill out your evangelism journal. Then go back through your journal and see how the Lord is moving in the hearts of your friends.

CHAPTER 10

Take Action to Be Counter Cultural

"Our business is to present the Christian faith clothed in modern terms, not to propagate modern thought clothed in Christian terms. Confusion here is fatal."

J. I. Packer

GET OUTSIDE OF YOURSELF AND THEM

"Just then His disciples came back. They marveled that He was talking with a woman, but no one said, 'What do you seek?' or, 'Why are you talking with her?'"

John 4:27

Jesus' encounter by the well dispels a common myth that many common bonds have to exist between both parties for witnessing to succeed. In fact, the vast differences between Jesus and this woman are revealed through her question, "How is it that you, a Jew, ask for a drink from me, a woman from Samaria" (John 4:9)? Men and women avoided conversation in public during that time. In fact, to converse with a woman in public was as offensive in nature as eating forbidden foods. Moreover, Jews hated Samaritans and avoided them because they had distorted the Jewish religion, holding only to the Pentateuch. Like Jesus, we must prayerfully find ways of being countercultural for the sake of the gospel. We do not want to be contrary, argumentative, or behave in ways that dishonor the message of the gospel. However, we must recognize that there are places in which we can be countercultural and in so doing share the gospel more fully.[1]

Jesus also dispelled another common myth: a long relationship must be established in order to gain a hearing for the gospel. Jesus initiates a conversation with a person, and then within minutes (if not seconds) is already into a very productive conversation about spiritual matters. Similarly, we must be careful not to assume that we must befriend someone before sharing the gospel. On the contrary, we must build every relationship we have on a foundation of our faith in Jesus. In this way, each person with whom we connect will know of our faith. There will be no need of finding other ways to bring Jesus into established relationships. This avoids the "bait and switch" idea that tells your Muslim friends you were not a true friend. This also avoids the temptation to continue waiting to introduce the gospel into the relationship since it has already been done. This might seem a bit strange, but simply stating at the beginning of the friendship that you are a follower of Jesus and then asking him what his beliefs are will quickly and unobtrusively lay the foundation for more discussions about Jesus.

Application

1. What are your feelings about friendship evangelism? How might they have changed after this teaching?
2. Brainstorm with your partner ways in which you can be countercultural for the sake of the gospel.
3. Pray together for your contacts. Discuss a plan of discipleship for those who have made a decision to follow Christ. Discuss a follow-up plan for those who have yet to come to that place of decision.

CHAPTER 11

Be a Bridge Builder

"Never pity missionaries; envy them. They are where the real action is—where life and death, sin and grace, Heaven and Hell converge."

Robert C. Shannon

YOU ARE A LIVING WITNESS OF THE GOSPEL

"So the woman left her water jar and went away into town and said to the people, 'Come, see a man who told me all that I ever did. Can this be the Christ?' They went out of the town and were coming to him."

John 4:28–30

One might be impressed by the short bridge Jesus used in witnessing by the well. The conversation is centered around a common need, and then quickly bridges into a relevant discussion about Jesus, the living water. However brief and direct the bridge is, it is very functional. It teaches us that everyday moments have eternal significance when the Holy Spirit is involved.

Application

1. Our message today was short and simple: be a bridge builder. The reason it is short is so you and your partner can take time to brainstorm and discuss potential bridges from daily life to the gospel. This might include things like noticing that even a toddler disobeys without being taught, showing original sin and the need for a way to God. Before you begin, pray together for the Holy Spirit to open your eyes to see how the mundane can be of eternal significance.
2. Read over your notes from previous meetings and discuss follow-up and discipleship plans.
3. Celebrate together by updating your evangelism tracker. See those who are drawing closer to Jesus, those who have made a decision to follow Christ and those who are on their way. Pray for each contact by name.
4. Prayerfully consider changing your partnership and each person finding someone new with whom to join. These new people should be those who have not gone through this training, but with whom you can each share this information. You may want the four of you to meet together for the training and then go out in pairs to meet Muslims as well as follow up on those with whom you have been previously meeting. In this way, you are able to reproduce yourselves and spread the gospel further.

- PART TWO -

Moving Forward

"The church changes the world not by making converts, but by making disciples."

John Wesley

Now that we have explored the nature of Islam and sharing the gospel with Muslims, we can move forward in bringing Muslims into communities of faith. The next three chapters give practical insights and wisdom for those seeking to disciple Muslim background believers (MBBs). This section of the book looks at the challenges MBBs face as well as how followers of Christ can come alongside them as they continue on their journey in Christ.

CHAPTER 12

Go and Make Disciples

"Christianity without discipleship is always Christianity without Christ."

Dietrich Bonhoeffer

TOPICS FOR EFFECTIVE DISCIPLESHIP

There is no easy way to disciple a Muslim background believer (MBB). It simply takes a lot of time, intentionality, and prayer. Be prepared. Your life is no longer your own. Just as new parents embrace sleeplessness and a change in schedule, discipling a new believer will take much of your time and energy.

There is a plethora of resources for discipleship available around the world in almost every language. Because of this, we will not reinvent the wheel, so to speak. Instead, an outline of topics is provided to aid in determining what system of discipleship you choose.[1]

There are basic challenges that every MBB faces. These challenges can be broken down into five main areas: spiritual, family and community, Islamic ideology and doctrine, sociopolitical, and psychological. Some of the issues fit more than one category. Each area represents issues relating to a MBB's growth in Christ and must be addressed at some point. When it is addressed, it is between you, the person, and the work of the Holy Spirit. Regardless of the system or method chosen for discipleship, the most important aspect is that it be Spirit-led. As disciplers, we can have the best program in the world, but unless the relationship with the believer is led by the Holy Spirit, it will be in vain. The Holy Spirit is the greatest teacher and knows areas of growth that need to be addressed.

With this in mind and in consideration of the issues MBBs face, these topics should be included in any discipleship program. Understand that this is by no means an exhaustive list.

FOUNDATIONAL SPIRITUAL GROWTH IN CHRIST

- Knowing and embracing that God is love and loves her/him
- Committing to and being involved in a community of faith
- Submitting to a trusted discipler who models the Christ-like life
- Valuing the Scripture and applying its teaching to her/his everyday life
- Growing in daily prayer both for her/his needs and the needs of others
- Receiving intentional teaching in doctrine and a moral life
- Sharing the gospel and discipling others
- Committing to obeying Christ at all costs
- Understanding and using spiritual gifts in life and ministry
- Confessing sin and asking for forgiveness
- Embracing persecution and opposition as part of life in Christ
- Worshiping the Lord in Spirit and in truth
- Understanding the function of the Holy Spirit
- Taking responsibility for her/his own growth in Christ rather than depending on others

FAMILY AND COMMUNITY

- Dealing with pressures from family in a Christ-like manner
- Trusting other believers
- Understanding biblical family life such as issues related to marriage and child rearing
- Forgiving other believers when they do not accept her/him as a follower of Christ
- Giving generously
- Embracing grace and rejecting shame
- Dealing with sexual issues and lust
- Having a bold God-vision for the faith community
- Recognizing that there is an enormous community of believers around the world
- Submitting to spiritual authority

ISLAMIC IDEOLOGY AND DOCTRINE

- Rejecting the Satanic hold of Islamic teaching and embracing the

truth of Jesus
- Recognizing God as near and knowable
- Establishing her/his identity in Christ rather than as a Muslim
- Embracing the role she/he plays in life rather than passive fatalism

SOCIOPOLITICAL

- Dealing with issues related to her/his official religion on an ID card
- Prayerfully determining when to tell her/his community of the decision to follow Christ

PSYCHOLOGICAL

- Processing through fear and utilizing the Scripture in response
- Living a life of freedom in Christ rather than in bondage

FEAR

At the core of almost every issue a MBB faces is fear. Many Muslim families and communities use fear to control members of their community. This fear leads to intimidation and becomes part of a Muslim's psyche causing him to wrestle with anything that might go against the wishes of his family and/or community. I remember a young woman I had been discipling. We had been reading the gospels together and she was insatiable for the things of Christ. However, after only a few weeks she came to me, and with tears in her eyes said that although she knew that what I was teaching was the truth from God, she could not become a follower of Christ. The cost would simply be too great. It would mean that her family would turn their backs on her and that was more than she could endure.

Because of the gravity of this issue, fear must be dealt with in a variety of ways and through a variety of instances with grace and truth. Those instances will arise as you continue to walk with your friend in his journey in Christ.

IDENTITY

When a Muslim professes her faith in Jesus, she is immediately placed in the middle of tug-of-war. On one side of the rope is her new Christian faith with grace, freedom, and love. On the other side of the rope is her old belief in Islam with its religiosity, legalism, family, and community. The more the new believer grows in Christ, the greater this tension builds. How does she now relate to her family and community?

We had a young man in a small faith fellowship. He had a powerful conversion experience that included a vision of Christ. He grew by leaps and bounds and was absolutely in love with Jesus. He even asked his believing friends to call him James, showing he had turned his back on Islam which included his Muslim name. However, his family did not know of his newfound faith. He developed two separate identities. One as a believer with a new name who read the Scriptures and prayed to Jesus, and the other with his old name who went to mosque with his father and participated in ritual prayers. When his family asked about his change in countenance, he shrugged it off mumbling something about being happy with his foreign friends. Eventually, it came time for his family to find him a wife. They did so according to their family belief system: a wife of a good, devout Muslim family. For a while, this young man continued his double life as a secret Christ follower. Eventually, though, as he became a father and took on more responsibility in his community, his Christian practices were neglected. He would now say he is only a Muslim and simply had a time of searching. He considers the births of his two sons as proof that God is pleased with his choice to remain a Muslim. He celebrated his sons' first time saying prayers in a mosque and took them on hajj to Mecca.

Sadly, this is all too common. New believers will often abandon their faith for what is familiar and comfortable. As a discipler, we must prayerfully discern our response to this. A follower of Christ has his identity solely in Christ. However, we are all on the path of learning this more. But truth must accompany grace as we navigate these tumultuous waters with our new believing friends. It is often one step forward, three steps back, two steps forward, ten steps back. The key is simply to journey through this together with the Holy Spirit's guidance.

Application

1. With your partner, research discipleship resources available to you and brainstorm how they might be used in working with Muslims. You might consider starting with Global Initiative (reachingmuslimpeoples.com). Their mission is to help the church minister to Muslim people.
2. With your partner, pray for your Muslim friends and ask the Lord for direction on the best method of ministering.

CHAPTER 13

Church Planting

"The church exists for nothing else but to draw men into Christ, to make them little Christs. If they are not doing that, all the cathedrals, clergy, missions, sermons, even the Bible itself, are simply a waste of time. God became man for no other purpose."

C. S. Lewis

In the words of John Lindell, lead pastor of James River Church in Springfield, Missouri, "our spiritual walk was not meant to be do-it-yourself. We were created for community." Regardless of cultural background, the Lord designed us to need the body of Christ. However, this is even more important for Muslims who come from a community-oriented culture.

When a Muslim comes to faith in Christ, she often finds herself very much alone; something she has never experienced before. I spoke with a friend once about the marriage her family arranged for her. She was bright and beautiful, and I as an American found the idea of being forced into a marriage abhorrent. I was put in my place when she answered my question of her feelings on it. She looked at me quizzically and said, "I trusted my family to choose the best school for me and the best university program for me. Why would I not trust them with the most important decision of my life?" For most Muslims, decisions are not made individually. Everything is collective. That is why developing a faith community is crucial to meeting this heartfelt need of MBBs.

There are basically three options as it relates to developing a faith community: a small group or house church, integrating the believer into a larger mainstream church, or a combination of the two.

DEVELOPING A SMALL GROUP OR HOUSE CHURCH

Living in the Arab world among Muslims, my desire is to bring new believers into community together to formulate small house churches. It makes the most sense. In the Arab world there simply aren't many mainstream churches for them to attend. The only option is developing something small, new, and very much like the early church. As with any church start-ups, there are pros and cons to consider:

PROS

- There are no Western Christian cultural traditions to break.
- The group is comprised of MBBs, all who can relate and encourage one another.
- The small size is easily managed regarding what is taught, how it is taught, and where the group is going.
- It is modeled in Scripture, so believers are able to understand the system well.

CONS

- Small groups can become isolated and insular.
- Small groups can be discouraging. Because the group is so small, it might seem like there are few believers.
- Small groups can become breeding grounds for interpersonal issues.
- Consideration must be given for children, youth, singles, etc.

INTEGRATION IN A MAINSTREAM CHURCH

There are many factors that play into whether integration is the best course of action for a Muslim believer. The first item to consider is the location of the church versus the person. Can he actually get to the building? Then, one must consider if the church members would be welcoming to a believer from a Muslim background. Finally, consideration should be given as it relates to the believer's family and how they might respond.

PROS

- The believer is immediately part of a large community of like-minded Jesus followers.
- The discipleship of believers can be spread out over many different people.
- There are other ministries for the believers to participate in.
- There are systems in place for children and youth.

CONS

- Sometimes church members are not welcoming to MBBs.
- Believers can become lost in the crowd if strategic plans are not in place.
- Believers may feel uncomfortable being seen walking into a church building.
- Mainstream churches have traditions and cultural components that may not be understood by MBBs.

COMBINATION OF SMALL GROUP AND INTEGRATION IN A MAINSTREAM CHURCH

Just as I believe that, aside from Jesus, no human is perfect, I believe no church or small group is either. Fallen humans comprise each one. It seems that for most believers, their best chance at growing into mature, reproducing believers is through multiple avenues. In the North American context, there is a unique opportunity to take advantage of both public worship and smaller, more intimate gatherings in homes. When we are leading Muslims to Jesus, we should consider how we can take advantage of both possibilities. By implanting a believer into the life of a mainstream church *and* providing a small group of like-minded people for fellowship, MBBs are given many opportunities to see Christ in action in the lives of other believers. They are able to develop community and have a better perspective on the size of the Kingdom of God. By utilizing both methods, many of the drawbacks to one or the other are dealt with. The most important thing is that a new community is created for the believer where she can feel a sense of belonging.

Some guidelines for integrating MBBs in both the mainstream church and in small groups includes the following:

- Have a conversation with your church leadership about your heart for Muslims and the desire to provide a forum that can reach more of them. Informing them of your desire on the front end helps them know how to pray for you and which resources of the church you need (i.e., literature, volunteers, meetings rooms, wider prayer, ideas, opportunities, etc.)

- Discuss with your church leaders their guidelines and wisdom for hosting a meeting in your house that functions as a small group, life group, or evangelism group for Muslims and MBBs. Ask the church if they want this to be a formal part of their small group structure or if they would prefer you do this more independently but in good communication with them.
- Keep your church leaders informed of testimonies, challenges, opportunities, and developments in the house group and work together with your church on longer-term developments. Talk with your church leaders about:

    1. How they want this house church connected to the public life of the church.
    2. If they would like to see church members start similar groups for other unreached peoples and how to go about doing that.
    3. How the church can make these MBBs welcome in public meetings *and integrate them into the life of the church*.
    4. If there can be private baptismal services with witnesses but not publicized, taking the security issues of MBBs into consideration.

Essentially, you want the blessing and spiritual support of your church leaders in whatever you do when it comes to leading Muslims to Jesus. You don't want to minister independently from the body of Christ and you want to see others in your church reach out to Muslims as well. In order for this to work, you need to be in constant, clear communication with your church leadership working with their favor and encouragement, while talking with them about growth and integration.

Depending on several factors (seekers, new believers, church vision and framework, the congregation), there will be a continuum of possibilities on the marriage between private and public community life for new believers. Most often private meetings will be an introductory step towards entry into the body of Christ, and then down the road, a supplementary step through contextual and relational intimacy, familiarity, and encouragement as believers are integrated into public church ministry. The critical thing is that you have a clear, open, agreed-upon plan and system with your church leadership.

Some churches will empower a meeting just for MBBs in their native language, but often that is only effective for the first generation of immigrants. Long-term integration into the greater church is the healthy direction and allows for new MBBs to reach into their families and friends who are still Muslims in vibrant and contextual gospel witness.

LEADERSHIP DEVELOPMENT

There is a Haitian saying that says, "It takes thirty years to grow a tree, but it takes one hundred years to grow a man." This speaks to the patience and intentionality required to disciple a MBB and to develop leadership qualities. Regardless of what method or system is chosen, the bottom line is that leaders are required for the work of discipling. No matter the size of the group, a leader, someone to take on the pastoral role, is needed. Eugene Peterson in his book, *From the Pastor: A Memoir*, says, "The only way the Christian life is brought to maturity is through intimacy, renunciation, and personal deepening. And the pastor is in a key position to nurture such maturity."[1] Be prepared to foster over the long haul the kinds of intimacy, renunciation, personal deepening, and authentic community that will result in healthy leaders for faith communities of MBBs. It will not be easy. But it will be eternally significant.

Application

1. With your partner, begin observing your church. Are there multiple ethnicities present? Would a MBB be welcome? How might you go about integrating someone into the life of your church? Be sure to talk with your pastor or leader about this.
2. If possible, invite a Muslim friend to your church. Be sure to explain what will happen so your friend will not be completely surprised. Observe their reactions to various parts of the service and how church members responded to them. Debrief with them afterwards. Ask what their favorite part was and if they have any questions.

CHAPTER 14

The Insider Movement

> "'You are no saint,' says the devil. Well, if I am not, I am a sinner, and Jesus Christ came into the world to save sinners. Sink or swim, I go to Him; other hope, I have none."
>
> *Charles Spurgeon*

"Insider Movement Missiology" (IMM)[1] is a term used for an approach in outreach to Muslims that claims people can genuinely be saved yet remain within their former religious community. According to IMM, a person can have dual religious identity—they can be a genuine follower of Jesus while continuing to participate in many, if not all, of their original religious practices.

Proponents of IMM love the lost and desire believers remain within their communities for the sake of witness. IMM proponents hold the conviction that believers do not have to exchange their cultural identity for another culture to follow Christ. While affirming these motivations, we find IMM to be unbiblical.

AFFIRMATIONS OF WHAT WE BELIEVE

In clarifying what we do find biblical, we make these affirmations:

1. That people from every tribe, tongue, people, and nation can trust in Jesus and be saved without rejecting their cultural or ethnic identity. We also affirm that aspects of every culture are fallen and Christ transforms all cultures.
2. That it is right for believers to express their faith within their own culture and indigenous churches. We affirm that indigenous believers and churches have the right and responsibility to develop their own theology as members of the body of Christ in mutual accountability.
3. That we pray for, desire, and work towards movements of peoples to Christ.
4. That believers should be encouraged to remain in their community and context whenever possible, to glorify God and advance the gospel.
5. That practitioners of the gospel should be sensitive and respectful towards local cultures and should adapt to them as much as possible,

without compromising what is taught by Scripture. We believe biblically guided contextualization is necessary and appropriate.
6. That there is no salvation apart from understanding, believing, and confessing faith in the gospel of Jesus Christ and that Jesus is God.
7. That the Bible, and the Bible alone, is the only book given by inspiration of the Holy Spirit. It alone is inerrant, and it is the only source of revelation from God. We do not recognize any other book as coming from God. The Bible sets non-negotiable boundaries to all of our efforts to contextualize the gospel.
8. That the message in evangelism and discipleship must be based on the Bible. Any references to the scriptures of other faiths should be made in such a way that does not give those writings any spiritual authority. We affirm that Christian theology—most crucially Christology—must be based on the Bible, not any other religious text.
9. That non-biblical religions do not save and cannot be used to express faith in Jesus Christ and that they are not neutral but rather oppress and suppress the truth. We affirm that other religions are the authority on their faith and practice and we cannot read Christian meanings into their religious texts.
10. That conversion out of false religion is a biblical requirement and expectation. Biblical conversion marks a radical break with our rebellious past, including all forms of unbiblical religion and entails identification with Christ and His historic and global people.

In light of these affirmations, we are therefore convinced that:

1. Ministers of the gospel should never give the impression that they have converted to another religion for any reason, even in order to become accepted in that religious community. And that while Christianity is unique and superior, it can be classified as a "religion" in that it pertains to belief in and about God as well as a way of life prescribed by God.
2. Believers in Jesus should never be taught that their former religion or its books, founders, or prophets are inspired by God.
3. Believers should never be encouraged to continue to practice their

former religion. For example, it is unbiblical to be a Muslim follower of Jesus.
4. Believers should be taught the crucial importance of the church, a local body of baptized believers in Jesus Christ, to their own life as disciples of Jesus.
5. Believers should be taught the crucial importance of being baptized in the Holy Spirit for empowerment to witness in word and that martyrdom as persecution is sure to follow conversion to Christ and solidarity with His body.
6. Believers and ministers should avoid any practice that would suggest a devotion to any god other than the Triune God of the Bible.

THE TERM "MUSLIM"

The term "Muslim" must be interpreted by Muslims, not by Christians. To be Muslim according to Muslims is to believe among other things that the Quran is the inspired and infallible word of God, that Mohammed is the prophet of God, and that "there is no God but God and Mohammed is the prophet of God" (the Islamic confession of faith, the *shahada*). Every Muslim would agree that you must affirm the above in order to be Muslim.

To reinterpret "Muslim" as merely someone submitted to God ignores the primary meaning of the word/term as understood by its owners and is therefore deceptive. It is impossible from the perspective of both religions (Islam or Christianity) to be a Jesus Muslim.

Christians do not believe that the Quran is inspired of God. Christians do not believe that Mohammed is the prophet of God. Christians, when they understand what the *shahada* is actually saying, cannot agree with it. Islam is an anti-Christ religion that denies the Father, Son,[2] and Holy Spirit.[3] When the Islamic creed (*shahada*) declares, "There is no God but God," it is denying Trinitarian monotheism. Thus, it is denying the deity of Jesus and the Holy Spirit. When the Islamic creed pronounces, "Mohammed is the prophet of God," it is denying that Jesus is the mediator between God and man. Properly understood, the Islamic creed proclaims five times a day from every mosque globally that *Jesus is not God, Jesus is not the mediator between God and man.*

No Christian can adopt an identity that is linked to Islam. The religions are antithetical to one another, for one is based on believing and proclaiming the deity of Jesus and one was formed and exists to deny that Jesus is God and the Savior of the world.

What is appropriate for ministers of the gospel, both Christian background believers and Muslim background believers, is a term/title/identity that is connected to Jesus. This does not have to be the word "Christian" as that term can be misunderstood, but it can be. Ultimately every term is problematic as terms tend to be defined by the behavior of the person claiming that term, and all persons are frail.

Examples of suitable terms include: follower of Jesus, disciple of Jesus, Jesus follower, lover of Jesus, servant of Jesus, follower of Christ, disciple of Christ, Christ follower, lover of Christ, servant of Christ, or any other combination that shows we are connected to Jesus in a subservient relationship. He is Lord, and we are His.

USE OF THE QURAN

An essential principle in contextualization is that we cannot insert the meanings of one religion into the religion of another. We cannot prove Christian theology through the Quran. We cannot witness from the Quran or give authority to the Quran. It is appropriate to know what the Quran says so we may be informed in presenting our biblical case, but we need to do so being aware that the intent of the Quran is to suppress and repress biblical truth about God, specifically the nature of Jesus.

The Quran says that that Jesus is "the word of God and a spirit from Him." It might seem that this statement buttresses incarnation theology and the deity of Jesus, but it actually does not. It is part of a corpus that categorically rejects the deity of Jesus or the incarnation. It is a violation of hermeneutics to read biblical meanings into Quranic texts by taking them out of context. Any reference to the Quran must avoid giving it authority. This is easily done by framing Quran references as questions and quickly transitioning to the Bible. For example, "Why does the Quran say that Jesus is the word of God and a spirit from Him? ...Ah, that is interesting because the Bible says..."

It is indeed helpful for the minister to know what the Quran says, but any reference to the Quran should be made fastidiously avoiding giving it authority. This is best done by framing the reference in a question and immediately transitioning to what the Bible says about Jesus and the character of God.

Application

The bottom line is to know the Word of God. We will get further in sharing the gospel with Muslims simply by focusing on Jesus.

The reality is that there are 2.5 million mosques around the world each denying Christ's deity five times each day. This means that Christ's deity is denied 12.5 million times each day. Our goal must be to lift Jesus up constantly.

With your partner:

1. Go through the Gospels and write down every attribute of Jesus you find.
2. Commit to asking your Muslim friends what their understanding of Jesus is. Then have them read the Gospels themselves (or just have them read the Gospel of Mark) and discuss what was read.
3. Journal about your meeting in your evangelism tracker.

Conclusion

"Some wish to live within the sound of the church or chapel bell.
I want to run a rescue shop within a yard of hell!"

C. T. Studd

The goal of this entire guide is for you to share the gospel with Muslims. This task seems overwhelming, like a mountain that can never be moved. But Jesus taught us that if we have the faith of a mustard seed, we can say to this mountain, "Move!" and it will be moved (Matt. 17:20). Through faith in Jesus and obedience to the Holy Spirit's direction, we can see Muslims come to salvation. It will be difficult. There will be times when you want to give up. But it can also be glorious as you watch a friend begin to discover that Jesus loves him. There is no greater privilege than participating in that beautiful journey.

SHARE THE GOSPEL

Remember to follow the steps outlined in previous chapters. Based on the *Any3* method,[1] the following summary includes some open-ended questions to help you share the gospel with Muslims.

1. **GET CONNECTED**

- Build rapport through small talk.
- Ask questions that will answer "How are you?" and "Who are you?"

2. **GET TO THE POINT**

- Transition to spiritual matters.
- Pray for an open door.
- If the open door doesn't immediately happen, say: "You follow Islam, right?"

3. **GET TO LOSTNESS**

- Reveal the common sin and shame problem and the frustration of failing in our religious duties by letting them talk about their religious experiences.
- Ask: "Almost all religions are the same, aren't they?"
- Ask: "Isn't the point of Islam to try to do good and be good enough to please God, so that God will receive us? It is concerned with doing

good things to offset our sins, but are the sins ever paid off?"
- We are all frustrated, aren't we? We try our best to please God, but failure (sin) continually which leaves us frustrated and ashamed.
- Ask: "We are all sinners (shameful), aren't we?"
- Ask: "Our sin debt gets larger instead of smaller because we sin every day, don't we?"
- Ask: "What are you doing to get your sins forgiven? Are your sins paid off yet? When will they be paid off? In eternity, will your sins be forgiven? How can you be sure?"

4. GET TO THE GOSPEL

- Say: "What I believe is different from that."
- My sins are already paid off, but not because of the good things I do. By the way, you're probably a better person than I am.
- My sins are paid off because God Himself made a way to forgive sins.
  1. Jesus came from heaven and was born of a virgin.
  2. Jesus lived a holy life.
     a. Jesus never sinned, although tempted.
     b. Jesus never married, was from the ordinary class rather than from the upper class, and early in His public ministry fasted for forty days and forty nights.
     c. Jesus performed mighty miracles, including raising people from the dead.
     d. Jesus began prophesying to His followers that He would surrender Himself to evil rulers, would be killed to pay for people's sins, and would rise again three days later.
        1. All of our forefathers gave blood sacrifices to have their sins forgiven (Adam and Eve, Cain and Abel, Noah, Abraham, and Moses).
        2. *The story of Adam and Eve:* One sin brought severe punishment from God although they had done many good deeds. God gave them animal skins showing that a blood sacrifice was needed to cover their sin and shame. John the Baptist proclaimed, "Behold the Lamb of God that takes

away the sin of the world." According to the Law, Prophets, Psalms, and the Gospels, "without the shedding of blood, there is no forgiveness of sins."

3. Jesus died to pay our sin debt, and then three days later He was raised from the dead, proving that God received Jesus' sacrifice.

4. The gospel says that if we believe Jesus paid for our sins with His death and surrender ourselves to Him as Lord, we will be saved.

5. *That's why I know my sins are forgiven, and it's not because I'm a better person than you, because I know you're probably a better person than me, but because of Jesus' sacrifice for my sin and shame.*

5. **GET TO A DECISION**

- If the person is not open to the gospel, share the gospel briefly and then change the subject. A door may open later, so be sure to continue following up.
- If she/he is open to the gospel:
  1. Invite her/him to receive Christ.
  2. Briefly tell her/him the other sacrifice stories.
  3. Invite her/him to invite friends to study the sacrifice stories.
  4. Make a plan for her/his discipleship and participation with a local fellowship.

CHALLENGES WILL ARISE

There are areas of difficulty as it relates to a Muslim coming to faith in Jesus. Once again, Global Initiative (reachingmuslimpeoples.com) has a number of resources available on its website that can help guide you in this area. One such challenge and possible responses are outlined below.

- *Question:* "I think God will forgive my sins because He is merciful."

  Answer: "God has said there is only one way He will forgive sins, that is through blood sacrifices."

  Be sure to have them read Matthew 26:28; Romans 5:8–9; Hebrews

CONCLUSION

9:16–19; Ephesians 1:7; Colossians 1:14; 1 John 1:7; and Revelation 1:5.

After sharing one or more of the sacrifice stories from the Old Testament (Adam and Eve, Cain and Abel, Noah, Abraham, or Moses) and emphasizing the necessity of blood sacrifice for the forgiveness of sins, tell the car illustration, or one like it:

"Suppose a person wants to buy a car. He usually makes a payment plan at the bank to pay a particular amount per month. Let's say I bought a car this way, but when it was time to pay the first month's payment, I didn't have enough money. So, I tried to find a way out on my own. I gathered up five chickens which I was raising to feed my family, and then took the chickens to the bank. Imagine walking into the bank with chickens. People are looking at you like you are weird, and you are embarrassed. Finally, the cashier calls your number, so you approach the counter with your chickens and lay them on the counter. Will he receive your chickens as payment for your car? Of course not. He will laugh, right? Why? Because the agreement for payment was money, not chickens. That's how it is with God. God has made an agreement with mankind that sins can only be paid through the shedding of blood. And Jesus shed His blood as the final and only way for people's sins to be forgiven."

KEYS TO EFFECTIVE EVANGELISM

1. Share the good news. Bridges are very important, but they are not the good news. The good news of Jesus Christ is powerful just by itself.
2. Think of "relational" evangelism rather than "friendship" evangelism.
   a) Share the gospel frequently. It usually takes three or four times for a person to hear the gospel before becoming a believer.
   b) Share the gospel early in the relationship. It is best if the topic of Jesus is part of the initial meeting.
   c) Be sensitive to the person's culture and religious environment.
3. Learn to share the good news everywhere, but especially while "hanging out." Make time for it. Be intentional.

4. As you are talking, pray in the Spirit for God to open a door to share. Then believe He will open that door. Take time to pray with your friend in front of him.
5. Don't be too selective about who you tell about Christ. You'll be surprised by who is open to the gospel and who the person of peace might be.
6. Draw the net. Healthy evangelism involves sowing and reaping. Sow frequently, and frequently attempt to draw the net.

Woe to me if I do not preach the gospel.
(1 Cor. 9:16)

APPENDIX A: *Evangelism Journal Entry*

The purpose of this journal is for the individual or pair to track where a contact is on his/her journey to Christ. In this way, the person can prayerfully determine next steps as he/she seeks to guide the Muslim on the journey to faith in Jesus.

The first section on the first page is for basic information. It is important to note that many Muslims have the same name. That's why we included space for a basic description of the individual. This can include occupation, marital status, age, identifying markers, and other descriptors that will aid in remembering exactly who the person is. Adding the location is vital because when analyzed with others also keeping journals, basic locations will surface that aid others in discovering where women or men meet together. For instance, if it is discovered that several women met in a particular coffee shop and another person discovers she has met several women in a coffee shop, coffee shops around the city might be a great place to meet Muslim women. However, if everyone frequents the exact same places, they will find they are meeting the same people and limiting the scope of their sowing. They might also find the proprietors of the location reticent to allowing them to continue frequenting their business.

The second section of the first page is for the initial meeting. This section is then repeated in every page thereafter. It is vital to write a description of what was discussed as soon as possible after the meeting ends. This aids the person in praying for the individual as well as praying for the guidance of the Holy Spirit for the next meeting. This is important because each contact is different and so requires a unique path of finding Christ. That being said, there are some larger methods that a contact may fit in. For instance, the person may be very educated and very devout, so a contextualized form of the gospel that walks him/her through lessons might be a good fit. Or maybe the person is illiterate and so oral stories will be the most effective. This is where the leading of the Holy Spirit and the collaboration with others becomes most important.

In each meeting, there should be a time of prayer together. In this time, the person should ask in what areas the contact he/she is sharing with needs prayer. It is important to explain that we pray in the name of Jesus and that Jesus answers prayer. At the first meeting, it will likely not be the time to go into the theology of prayer, but state it simply and then ask for prayer requests. As the meetings progress, the contact will discover that Jesus does indeed answer prayer which will allow him/her to see His power and bring him/her closer to Him.

It is unlikely that a person will meet with only one contact at a time. Because Muslim culture is communal, they are rarely alone. In this case, there should be one journal entry for each Muslim that was present. This is because each person is different and will have his/her own journey for finding Christ.

It is likely that at some point an individual will drop off for a bit and not be willing to meet. Or that individual will become more devout in Muslim faith and practice. Do not be discouraged. It is during these times the Holy Spirit is doing a great work in the heart. Keep praying for him/her regularly. Allow some space. Then prayerfully discern when and how to contact that person again to reestablish the relationship. Just as you are pursuing each one, so the Holy Spirit is pursuing them.

EVANGELISM JOURNAL ENTRY

Name:
Date Met: *Location:*
Contact Information:
Basic Description:

- FIRST MEETING -

Who was present:

What was discussed:

Prayer requests:

Thoughts for next meeting:

Next meeting time and place:

NEXT MEETING

Date:

Who was present:

What was discussed:

Prayer requests:

Thoughts for next meeting:

Next meeting time and place:

Notes:

- NEXT MEETING -

Date:

Who was present:

What was discussed:

Prayer requests:

Thoughts for next meeting:

Next meeting time and place:

Notes:

APPENDIX B: *Discipleship Tracking Chart*

The purpose of the Discipleship Tracking Chart is to help you see where various individuals are in conversation, where they have come from, and where they are going to.[1] There are various columns. The purpose of each column is outlined below.

1. Sowing

Add the name of any individual you have met and with whom you have begun the process of sharing the gospel in this column. This could include a gospel presentation such as the Jesus film, a simple message of who Jesus is, or the like. Jesus' conversation with the Samaritan woman in John 4:7-27 is an example of sowing. This column will hold the most names and some may never move from this initial column.

2. Watering

Place the names of those who are being regularly exposed to the gospel in this column. These people are unlikely to be in a Bible study. Where the sowing column lists the hearers of the Word, this column lists the seekers of the Word. These are those Muslims who desire more information about Jesus and the gospel. An example of a watering activity would be Jesus' two days of teaching in the Samaritan town of Sychar from John 4:39–42. Placing an arrow next to the individual's name will indicate if he appears to be moving forward toward deeper faith in Jesus or is losing interest.

3. Reaping

Place the names of those who have made a decision to follow Christ but are not yet in a local fellowship in this column. Draw an arrow next to her name if she is moving forward in her faith or losing interest.

4. Keeping

This column is for the ones who have professed faith in Jesus and are in a local fellowship. It is broken into two categories: Committed and Co-Worker. The Committed column is for those who have been baptized and have joined a local fellowship. The Co-Worker column is for those who are now leaders within the local fellowship and/or laboring with others to see Muslims come to faith.

DISCIPLESHIP TRACKING CHART

Date: _____

SOWING Hearing the Word	WATERING In Bible Study	REAPING In Christ	KEEPING In Local Church	
			CORE	COMMITTED

- ENDNOTES -

PART 1
1. See Matt. 10:1–42; Mark 6:7–11; Luke 9:1–6; 10:1–24.

CHAPTER 1
1. See Quran 55:15. This is in contrast to man's creation from clay.
2. The *Kaaba* is the cubed structure in Mecca which is the focal point of their prayers each day.
3. Muslims call the Torah the *Tawrat* and consider it a sacred text.
4. Muslims call the Psalms *Zabur* and it is considered a sacred text.
5. Muslims believe Jesus wrote one book, the Gospel, and call it the *Injil*. They are generally unfamiliar with the idea of there being four books written by four different authors, none of whom was Jesus.
6. Tradition says that the 124,000 prophets or messengers were sent over the course of human history, the first being Adam and the last being Mohammad, with the others coming in between. There has been no research or scientific inquiry regarding this.
7. See Quran 14:4. It is important to understand there is a belief that Allah can and does cause people to sin.
8. The origin of the concept of jihad is found in the following Quranic passages: 2:190–193; 9:5, 13, 29. These verses permit fighting to ensure freedom for the worship of Allah.

CHAPTER 2
1. Mike Shipman. *Any-3: Anyone, Anywhere, Any Time – Win Muslims to Christ Now!* (Monument, CO: WIGTake Resources, 2013).

CHAPTER 4
1. See Matt. 10:7–16 and Luke 10:5–7.

CHAPTER 6

1. I, personally, do not use the Quran in sharing the gospel. I do not want anyone to assume I am giving the Quran any authority as a holy text. It is not holy or authoritative. Also, I would not want a Muslim interpreting the Bible and in so doing, twist its meaning. Thus, I cannot interpret the Quran through my Christian lens in hopes of leading someone to Christ. To do so would not only be disingenuous but also would be trying to build a house of faith on a foundation of lies. It simply does not work. The gospel is offensive. It offends everyone everywhere at some point. We must not shy away from that but believe that even so, the gospel is true and so must be preached it its entirety without apology. For more on this, see Chapter 14.

CHAPTER 10

1. A wise missionary to Muslim Arabs once said that our job is to make Jesus attractive. It is for this reason we must dress appropriately and for the most part follow cultural boundaries. However, we must also remember that we are not Muslims and so should be sure that no one identifies us as such but as the followers of Jesus we are.

CHAPTER 13

1. A more in-depth study on methods relating to discipling MBBs can be found in Don Little's book, *Effective Discipling in Muslim Communities*.

CHAPTER 14

1. Eugene Peterson. *From the Pastor: A Memoir* (New York: Harper Collins, 2011), 157–159.

CHAPTER 15

1. This chapter is taken from author and veteran missionary Dick Brogden's thoughts on Insider Movement Missiology. Used with permission.
2. "Who is the liar but he who denies that Jesus is the Christ? This is

the antichrist, he who denies the Father and the Son" (1 John 2:22).
3. In the teachings of Islam (see Quran 2:97; 16:102; 19:17; and Bukhari 1:8:345), the Holy Spirit is portrayed as the angel Gabriel, denigrating a member of the Holy Trinity to a created being. According to Ansar Al 'Adl in his article, "Angel Gabriel and the 'Holy Spirit,'" it is "unanimously agreed upon by all Muslim scholars" that the term "'Holy Spirit' is simply another title of Angel Gabriel."

CONCLUSION
1. Mike Shipman. *Any-3: Anyone, Anywhere, Any Time – Win Muslims to Christ Now!* (Monument, CO: WIGTake Resources, 2013).

APPENDIX B
1. The original chart, entitled Church Planting Tracking and Analysis Chart, was developed for Live Dead teams so that teams could get a "snapshot" of the work the team is doing as a whole. Here it is being developed as a tool for individuals to use for the various Muslims with whom they are ministering.

SOURCES & RECOMMENDED READING

Adeney, Miriam. *Daughters of Islam: Building Bridges with Muslim Women*. Downers Grove, IL, IVP, 2002.

Addison, Steve. *Movements that Change the World: Five Keys to Spreading the Gospel*. Downers Grove, IL: Intervarsity Press, 2011.

Fleming, David. *Contextualization in the New Testament: Patterns for Theology and Mission*. Downers Grove, IL: InterVarsity Press, 2005.

Malek, Sobhi. *Islamic Exodus: Into the Freedom of Christ*. Sacramento, CO: ISBS, 2014.

Peterson, Eugene. *From the Pastor: A Memoir*. New York: Harper Collins, 2011.

Piper, John. *Let the Nations Be Glad: The Supremacy of God in Missions*, 3rd ed. Grand Rapids, MI: Baker Academic, 2010.

Ripken, Nik. *Insanity of Obedience*. Nashville, TN: B&H Publishing, 2014.

Shipman, Mike. *Any-3: Anyone, Anywhere, Any Time – Win Muslims to Christ Now!*. Monument, CO: WIGTake Resources, 2013.

Sinclair, Daniel. *A Vision of the Possible*. Colorado Springs, CO: Biblica Publishing, 2005.

Smith, Steve and Ting Kai. *T4T*. Monument, CO: WIGTake Resources, 2011.

Strong, Cynthia and Meg Page. *A Worldview Approach to Ministry Among Muslim Women*. Pasadena, CA: William Cary Library, 2006.

Yoon, Sung Sug. *Identity Crisis: Standing Between Two Identities of Women Believers from Muslim Backgrounds in Jordan*. Eugene, OR: Wipf & Stock, 201

ACKNOWLEDGEMENTS

I first want to express my deep gratefulness to my Lord, Jesus Christ. Without Him I am nothing. I would also like to thank my husband, Adam, who continually encourages me to reach new heights. To my family, thank you for listening to my endless babble about ministry to Muslims. To Dick and Jennifer Brogden, thank you for your leadership, love, and patience. To our supporters, we could not do what we do without you. To those who also share the gospel with Muslims, I am thankful for your commitment to the task and look forward to the day when we can say the work is finished and Jesus is glorified.

Also Available from
LIVE | DEAD

The Live Dead Journal ▶

◀ **Live Dead The Journey**

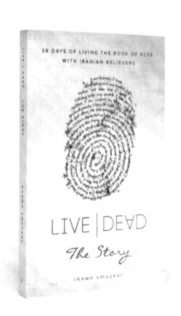

Live Dead The Story ▶

◀ **Live Dead Joy**

The Live Dead Journal:
Her Heart Speaks ▶

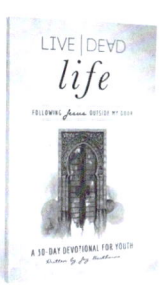

◀ ***Live Dead Life***

Live Dead India:
The Common Table ▶

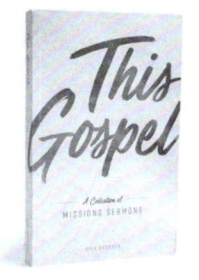

◀ ***This Gospel***

Diario Vivir Muerto ▶

Check out the full line of Live Dead devotionals
in the Live Dead online store at *livedead.org*.